The Philosophy of Hinduism

The Philosophy of HINDUISM

And Other Essays

DR. S. RADHAKRISHNAN

SINCE 1903

MOTILAL BANARSIDASS
PUBLISHING HOUSE

Second Reprint: Delhi, ***2025***
First Edition: Delhi, 1998

Also available at:
MOTILAL BANARSIDASS PUBLISHING HOUSE

- 4637/20, F-2, Hari Sadan, First Floor, Ansari Road, Darya Ganj Delhi–110 002 *Tel.*: (+91-11) 4559 7999
- 1st Floor, 1/2 Rathnavilas Road, Basvanagudi, Next to Pai Vista Convention Hall, South End Circle, Bengaluru–560004 (India) *Tel.*: +91-80-41275911

ISBN: 978-93-5760-284-6 (Hardcover)
ISBN: 978-93-5760-226-6 (Paperback)

Printed & Published by
Rajendra P Jain *for*
Motilal Banarsidass Publishing House
A-44, Naraina Industrial Area, Phase I, New Delhi–110 028 (INDIA)
Email: naraina@mlbd.in Website: www.mlbd.in
Tel.: (+91-11) 4751 1592

ACKNOWLEDGEMENTS.

THE PHILOSOPHY OF HINDUISM.
(The Hibbert Journal.)

THE HINDU DHARMA.
(The international Journal of Ethics.)

ISLAM AND INDIAN THOUGHTS.
(The Indian Review.)

HINDU THOUGHT AND CHRISTIAN DOCTORINE.
(The Madras Christian College Magazine.)

BUDDHISM.
(The Prabuddha Bharata.)

INDIAN PHILOSOPHY.
(Reprint 'Indian Philosophy'.)

CONTENTS

THE PHILOSPHY OF HINDUISM

I Propose in this paper to describe, not defend, the central features of the faith of Hindus, so as to bring out in a short compass its different sides of philosophical doctrine, religious experience, ethical character, and traditional faith.

Philosophical Basis

The Hindu religion is marked by an eminently rational character. Throughout the bewildering maze of dreamy hopes and practical renunciation, straitest dogmas and reckless adventures of spirit, throughout the four or five millenniums of ceaseless metaphysical and theological endeavour, the Hindu thinkers have tried to grapple with the ultimate problems in a spirit of loyalty to truth and feeling for reality. The Bramanical civilisation is so called since it is directed by the Brahmin thinkers, trained to judge issues without emotion and base their conclusions on the fundamentals of experience.

The feature of the world which led the Hindu thinkers to raise the question of the real was its passing away. The world open to our objective vision seemed to them an endless surpassing of itself. They asked, 'Is this passing away all, or does the doom which engulfs things meet its chech anywhere ?' And they answered, 'there is something in the world which is not superseded, an imperishable Absolute, Brahman'. This experience of infinity is given to all on some occasions, when we catch glimpses of the mighty secret, and feel the brooding presence of the larger self which mantles us in glory. Even in the tragic moments of life when we feel ourselves to be poor and orphaned, the majesty of the God in us makes us feel that the wrong and the sorrow of the world are but incidents in a greater drama which will end in power, glory and love.

The Upnishads declare, "If there were no spirit of joy in the Universe, who could live and breathe in this world of life ?" Philosophically, the real is the self-identical *Brahman* revealing itself in all, becoming the permanent background of the world-process. Religiously it is envisaged as the Divine Self-Conciousness, pregnant with the whole course of the world, with its evolutions and involutions. Throughout its long career, the oneness of the ultimate spirit has been the governing ideal of the Hindu religion. The Rigveda tells us of one Supreme Reality, *Ekam sat*, of which the learned speak variously. The Upnishads make out that the one *Brahman* is called by many names, according to function. The conception of *Trimurti* arises in the epic period, and is well established by the age of the puranas. The analogy of human consciousness, with its threefold activity of cognition, emotion, and will, suggests the view of the Supreme as *sat*, *chit* and *ananda* - reality, wisdom, and joy. The three gunas of *sattva* or equanimity, born of wisdom, *rajas* or energy, which is the outcome of spirited feeling, and *tamas* or heaviness, due to lack of enlightment and control, are aspects of all existence, and even God is not considered to be an exception to this law of the triplicity of all being. The three functions of *srishti* or creation, *sthiti* or maintenance, and *laya* or destruction are traced to the three gunas of rajas, sattva, and tamas. *Vishnu*, the preserver of the Universe, is the Supreme Spirit dominated by the quality of rajas; Satta,

Brahma creator of the universe is the supreme ominated by the quality of Rajas and Siva, the destroyer of the Universe, is the Supreme dominated by the quality of tamas. The three qualities of the one Supreme are developed into three distinct personalities, and each of the latter is said to function through its own respective *sakti* or energy, and so we have answering to Brahma, *Vishnu* and *Siva, Saraswati Lakshmi* and *Kali.* Strictly speaking, all these qualities and functions are so well balanced in the one Supreme that it cannot be said to possess any quality at all. (1) The one incomprehensible God who is omniscient, omnipresent and omnipotent appears to different minds in different ways. (2) An ancient text says that forms are given to the formless Absolute for the benefit of the aspirants.

With the openness of mind charactersitc of the philosophical temper, the Hindus believe in the relativity of the creeds to the general character of the people who profess them. Religion is not a mere theory of the supernatural which we can put on or off as we please. It is an expression of the spiritual experience of the race, a record of its social evolution, an integral element of the society in which it is found. That different faiths is not unnatural. It is all a question of taste and temperament. *Ruchinam vaichitryat.*

When the Aryans met the natives of the soil, who were worshipping all sorts of deities, they did not feel called upon to supplant their faiths all on a sudden. After all, all men are seeking after the one Supreme. According to the Bhagavadgita, God will not refuse the aspirant's wishes simply because they have not felt the power of His highest nature. Any attempt at a rapid passage from one set of rules to and other would involve a violent breach with the past, and consequently confusion and chaos. The great teachers of the world who possess a suffucient sense of the historical do not attempt to save the world in their own generation by forcing their advanced notions on those who cannot understand or appreciate them. Even so exacting an ethical teacher as Jesus implicitely justified Moses for legally demanding from the Israelites something less in the matter of divorçe than the highest ideal required - because of the hardness of their hearts. Look at the uncompromising words of Mars x. 11 ff. and Luke svi. 18, and the saving clauses introduced in Matthew (v. 32 and viv. 9.)

The Hindu thinkers, while they themselves practised a very high ideal, understood the unreadiness of the people for it and so took to careful tending instead of wild forcing. They admitted the lower gods, whom the masses ignorantly worshipped, and urged that they were all subordinate to the one Supreme. "While some men find their gods in the waters, others in the heavens, others in the objects of the world, the wise find the true God whose glory is manifest everywhere, in the heart, the feeble-minded in the idol, and the strong in his spirit finds God everywhere.(3)

Hindu systems of philosophy and religion recognise the periodical evolution and involution of the world representing the *diastole* of the one universal heart, which is ever at rest and ever active. The whole world is a manifiestation of God. *Sayana* observes, that all things whatsoever are vehicles for the manifestation of the supreme spirit.(4) These beings are distinguished into different grades. "Amongst beings, those that breathe are high; amongst these they that have developed mind; among them those that use their knowledge; while the highest are those who are possessed by the sense of the unity of all life in

Brahman". (5) The one foundational spirit is revealing itself throughout these divergence of form.

The infinite in man is not satisfied by the fashion of the finite world that passes away. Our troubles are due to the fact that we do not realise the God in us. Freedom is our possession, if we escape from all that is transient and finite in us. The more our life manifests the infinite in us, the higher are we in the scale of beings. The most intense manifestations are called the avatars or the incarnations of God. These are not out of the way, miraculous revelations of God, but only higher manifestations of the supreme principle, differing from the lower general ones in degree only. The Gita says, though God lives and moves in all, He manifests Himself in a special degree in things which are splendid. The Rishis and the Buddhas, the Prophets and the Messiahs, are intense revelations of the universal self. The Gita holds out a promise that they will appear whenever they are needed. When the downward materialist tendency dominates life, a Rama or a Krishna, a Buddha or a Jesus comes upon the scene to restrore the disturbed harmony of righteousness.

In these men who break the power of sense, unseal the heart of love, and inspire us with a love of truth and righteousness, we have intense concentrations of God. They reveal to us the way, the truth, and the life. They of course forbid the blind worship of themselves, since it retards the realisation of the great self. Rama considers himself to be nothing more than a son of man. (6) A Hindu who knows anything of his faith is ready to offer homage and reverence to all helpers of humanity. He believes that God may be incarnated in any man, even as He was in Jesus or Buddha. If the Christian thinkers admit that men may have access to God and be saved, other than through the mediatorship of Jesus, the Hindu will heartily subscribe to the essential features of the religion of Jesus. The divine manifestation is not an infringement of man's personality. On the contrary, it is the highest possible degree of man's natural self-expression, since the true nature of man is divine.

The aim of life is the gradual revelation in our human existence of the eternal in us. The general progress is governed by the law of Karma, or moral causation. The Hindu religion does not believe in a God who from his judgement-seat weighs each case separately and decides on its merits. He does not administer justice from without, enhancing or remitting punishment according to his sweet will. God is *in* man, and so the law of Karma is organic to man's nature. Every moment man is on his trial, and every honest effort will do him good in his eternal endeavour. The character that we build will continue into the future until we realise our oneness with God. The children of God in whose eyes a thousand years are as a day, need not be disheartened if the goal of perfection is not attained in one life. Rebirth is accepted by all Hindus. The world is sustained by our errors. The forces that integrate creation are our broken lives which require to be renewed. The Universe has appeared and disappeared times without number in the long past, and will continue to be dissolved and reformed through unimaginable eternities to come.

Religious Experience :
The effort of religion is to enable man to realise the divine in him, not merely as a formula or a proposition, but as the central fact of his being, by growing into oneness with it. The way to reach this religious experience cannot be

prescribed. The soul of man whose nature is infinite has unlimited possibilities in it. The God whom it seeks is equally infinite and wide. The reactions of an infinite soul to an infinite enviroment cannot be reduced to limit forms. The Hindu thinkers recognise that the exhaustless variety of life cannot be confined to fixed moulds. A familiar text declares: "As the birds float in the air, as the fish swim in the sea, leaving no traces behind, even so are the paths to God traversed by the seekers of spirit". (7) The Rishis of the Upanishads, the Prophets of Israel, and the founders of religions have heard God's voice and felt His presence. God is supremely impartial to His devotees, whatever form of address and approach they may adopt. "Whoever comes to me through whatsoever form, I reach him," says the Lord in the Gita.

However, distinctions are made on the basis of threefold activity of human consciousness, into the *Jnanamarga*, or the path of knowledge and illumination, *Bhaktimarga*, or the parth of faith and devotion, and *Karmamarga*, or the path of work and service. Thought, feeling, and will are not isolated faculties, but only distinguishable aspects of experience. Each of them makes its own contribution to the whole, and is penetrated by the others. The three-right knowledge, right desire, and right action-go together. The first reveals to us the truth, the second instils a love for it; and the third moulds life. Mere knowledge, unvivified by the warmth of feeling, leads to icy coldness of heart; mere emotion, unlit by knowledge, is hysteria; mere action, unguided by wisdom and uninspired by love, is meaningless ritual or feverish unrest. All the three enter into the integral experience of a perfect life. Yet as the emphasis on the three sides is changing in different men, they approach the problem of life from different sides.

The Gita says, "There is no purifier like unto *Jnana*, or wisdom." "This *Jnana* is not dialectical learning, which is dismissed as mere "words" in the famous dialogue in the Upanishads between Narada, the representative of encyclopaedic learning, and Sanatkumara, the true knower of the self. Man in his essential nature is freedom of spirit and wisdom. Our limitations shut us away from the reality of ourselves and subject us to error. The real question for logic is not, how or why the individual knows, but how or why he fails to know? Error is due to our limitations. Intellectual growth consists in breaking down these limitations when we directly experience reality. This kind of *Jnana*, which is independent of symbols and senses, is life living itself in the very heart of reality. Conceptual construction and logical learning may be useful in leading us to the true wisdom. The Gita insists on an intuitive insight, accompanied by rational knowledge *jnanam vijnana sahitam*. Without this logical support, intuition may turn out to be mere emotional subjectivity. The author of the Gita, by his saying clause, suggests that the direct consciousness of reality has universality about it. We can attain this experience of reality by a prayerful attitude. If we kill our intellectual conceit and acquire a receptive frame of mind, we shall lay ourselves open to the breeze from heaven. The Yoga discipline is intended to train the mind to hear the mighty voice of the silence within. We then feel our identity with the universal self, the Atman in us.

The cognative pursuit of God is rather slow and painful. "The Father and Maker of this whole it is hard to find, and when one has found Him, to declare Him to all his impossible."(8) Our life is so short and the search is so slow. We cannot afford to wait. We are in a hurry to see.

We wish to accept some faiths which will sustain us in life and help us to go about, free from doubt, acting and achieving. The impatience of the people to reach God is the opportunity for the quack who promises speedy salvation to those who believe in him. Supestition and magic become the daily bread of common people. In the Brahmanical system, reason does not completely abdicate. The sense of truth controls the life of the people. The highest truths of philosophy are dressed up in fables and stories, intelligible to the ordinary understanding that "all may safely cross beyond the difficult and dangerous places of life, that all may see the face of happiness, that all may attain to right knowledge, and all may rejoice everywhere."(9) The stories of the puranas enable the weak of mind to appreciate the highest good, and help the building up of the inner spirit.

Accepting all the forms of worship that prevailed in the country, the Hindu thinkers arranged them in a scale leading to the highest form of divine worship, which is the practice of the presence of God. A verse in the Siva purana reads, "The highest state is the natural realisation of God's presence, the second in rank is mediation and contemplation, the third is the worship of symbols which are reminders of the Supreme, and the fourth is performance of ritual and pilgrimages to sacred places." (10)

Idol-worship is unknown in the Rigveda. It obviously came into vogue later. It has always been recognized to be relative to an imperfect stage of development. Man is anthropomorphic, and is inclined to conceive God in vivid and pictorial form. He cannot express his mental attitude except through symbolism and art. However inadequate the symbols may be as expressions of the real, they are tolerated so long as they help the human spirit in its effort after the Divine. The symbol need not be superseded so long as it suggests the right standpoint.

There is a beautiful defence of image-worship, quoted from Maximus of Tyre, in Prof. Gilbert Murray's *Four Stages of Greek Religion*, which excellently sums up the Hindu's attitude to symbolic worship: "God Himself, the father and fashioner of all that is, older than the Sun or the sky, greater than time and eternity, and all the flow of being, is unnameable by any lawgiver, unutterable by any voice, not to be seen by any eye. But we, being unable to apprehend His essence, use the help of sounds and names and pictures, of beaten gold and ivory and silver, of plants and rivers, mountain peaks and torrents, yearning for the knowledge of Him, and in our weakness naming all that is beautiful in this world after His nature - just as happens to earthly lovers. To them the most beautiful sight will be the actual lineaments of the beloved, but for remembrance sake they will be happy in the sight of a lyre, a little spear, a chair pehaps, or a runnning ground, or anything in the world that awakens the memory of the beloved. Why should I further examine and pass judgement about Images ? Let men know what is divine, let them know; that is all. If a Greek is stirred to the remembrance of God by the art of Pheidias, an Egyptian by paying worship to animals, another man by a river, another by fire - I have no anger for their divergences; only let them know, let them love, let them remember."(11) These words so true, so tender, and so tolerant, jar on our ears, accustomed to hear dull dogmatics and fanatic falsehoods. If the symbolic function of the idol is overlooked, and if the metaphor is taken literally, the true God whom we are seeking to realise appears as He is not. The thinking Hindu does not forget the instrumental character of idol worship. The Yogies see God in Self and not in the images. (12)

Realising as it does the force of the lower forms of worship on the principle of milk for babes and meat for men, Hinduism has developed a religious atmosphere permeated by the highest philosophic wisdom as well as symbolic worship, round which much glorious art has gathered. It has room for all men of all grades of cultural equipment and religious instinct. In a Hindu home the most purified modes of worship retain some external form for the sake of the young who are growing up under the same roof. It is idle to stifle the impulses of the child by breaking its playthings, simply because we are grown up and do not find any need for them.

The emotionally-toned men look upon God as the perfect Beauty or Love, and wish to be lost in the enjoyment of His presence. Krishna is the typical God of beauty and love, and his appeal to men and largely women, dominated by emotion and sentiment, is great. A touching folk-song says, *"His flute doth call and I must go; and though the way be through the forest thick with thors, I must go."* When the irresistible call comes, none with a heart can fail to respond. For the aesthetic temperament, emotional intensity seems to give ultimate satisfaction. Beauty is its own excuse for being. The devotee clings to the feet of the Lord and refuses to leave them for anything on earth. Tukaram says, "I have grasped thy feet, I will not let them go... I will not let thee go, nor if thou givest me all else." Chaitanya says, "I crave not for money, nor for men, nor for a beautiful woman, nor for poetic genius. O Lord of the world, I only crave that in every birth of mine, bhakti may grow in me towards thee, O Lord." The Hindu thinkers combat the tendency to exalt religious devotion over love of truth and practice of goodness. They know full well that emotions are not isolated functions. By themselves they are morally colourless. The value of an emotion depends on the source from which it springs, whether it is an exalted spiritual devotion or a degrading sensual indulgence. The *bhakti* doctrine does not say that all feeling is sacred. Only the feeling of contemplative humility which accompanies the consciousness of absolute dependence on God is the true religious feeling or *bhakti*. Such a feeling expressive of knowledge issues in a life devoted to the service of man. Worship, music and art develop the religion of feeling.

The practically minded man tries to realise his divine destiny by the performance of duty, *karma*, and social service, *yajna*. Freedom is the nature of man; bondage is due to the barriers that shut us from ourselves. Our slavery is complete when we begin to hug it. If we break our selfishness, which walls us off from the world, and identify ourselves with the larger ends, we can gradually develop the love that casteth out fear, disarms all hatred, and breaks all springs of bitterness. Mere mechanical morality is not likely to lead us to the end. It has to be fed by a vital union with God. Then shall we realise that in every man there is a ray of the eternal light emanating from the Central Sun. When we love man, we are conscious of our unity with him in the central spirit and we give effect to this consciousness in our lives. This takes us to the next topic of the ethical charater of the Hindu religion.

Ethical Character :

The ethical discipline, which is an application of the doctrine to life, is intended to enable man to realise his potentialities, that he might stand secure in his own soul, free from the hold of the past and fearless of the chances of the future. Ethical endeavour consists in an attempt to live on earth, every moment of our life, in the sweet spirit of adoration, in the glad, consciousness of an eternal relatioship with God. The ideal man lives always in the light of heaven, and his life embodies the great vitrues of truth, purity, love and renunciation. Moral progress is judged not by man's power over the forces of nature, but by his control over the passions of the heart. To speak the truth under a shower of bullets, to refrain from reprisals even when you are on the Cross, to respect man and animal, to give all we have, to toil for others, and turn the other cheek, are the pricipal duties of man. Our modern practical reformers may dismiss them all as too high and unfit for becoming human nature's daily food, admirable ideals fit to console the feeble minds of Idia or the fishermen of Galilee, but impossible of realisation. Aware of the distance separating actual human nature from this ideal perfection, the Hindu thinkers devised a system of culture and discipline to train the individual for his destiny. The complex of institutions and influences which shape the moral feeling and character of the people is called the *dharma*, which is a fundamental feature of the Hindu religion. Hinduism does not believe in enforcing creeds, but calls upon all Hindus to conform to the discipline. It is a culture more than a creed. If ye do the will or the dharma, ye shall know of the doctrine or the truth. The dharma helps the smouldering fire which is in every individual to burst into flame.

The *dharma* is a code of conduct supported by the general conscience of the people. It is not subjective in the sense that the conscience of the individual imposes it, nor external in the sense that the law enforces it. It is the system of conduct which the general opinion or the spirit of the people supports, what the Germans call *sittlichkeit.* Fiehte defines the latter as "those principles of conduct which regulate people in their relations to each other, and have become matter of habit and second nature at the stage of culture reached, and of which therefore we are not explicitly conscious." The dharma does not force men into virtue, but trains them for it. It is not a fixed code of mechanical rules, but a living spirit which grows and moves in response to the development of the society. Even the State in India was a servant of the dharma. It was not above morality. Its function was not to alter or annual dharma, but only to administer it. The functions of the State never intruded into the life of the people. The dharma or the social life has continued the same in principle for over 4000 years in spite of divergent religious creeds, dynastic wars, and political feuds. The living continuity of Indian life is to be seen not in her political history, but in her cultural and social life. Political obsession has captured India since the battle of Plassey. To-day politics have absorbed life. The State is invading society, and the India of "no nations," as Rabindranath puts it, is struggling to become a "nation" in the Western sense of the term, with all its defects and merits.

The *dharma* has two sides, which are inter-dependent, the individual and the social. The conscience of the individual requires a guide and he has to be taught the way to realise his pupose and live according to spirit and not sense. The interests of society require equal attention. Dharma is that which holds together all living beings in a harmonious order.(13) Virtue is conduct contributing to social welfare, and vice is its opposite. It is frequently insisted that the highest virtue consists in doing to others as we would be done by. Both the individual and the social virtues are included in what are called *nitya karmas*, or obligatory duties, which are cleanliness or *shaucham*, good manners or *acharam*, social *service* or *panchamahyajnas*, and prayer and worship or *sandyavandanam*. The *varnasrama dharma*, which deals with the classes of society and the stages of the individual life, develops the details.

The end of the individual is not so much the securing of happiness here on earth as the realisation of an ideal, the accomplishment of a mission. This has to be achieved through the education of the individual, which ivolves restraint and sufferig. Four stages are distinguished in each man's life. In the first stage of *Brahmacharya*, the obligations of temperance, sobriety, chastity, social service are firmly established in the minds of the young. All have to pass through this discipline, irrespective of class or rank, wealth or poverty. In the second stage of a Grihasta or householder the individual undertakes the obligations of family life. He becomes a member of a social body and accepts its rights and obligations, some of the sweetest of the habits of human nature are developed through the ties that bind us to our fellow-men. Self-support, thrift, and hospitality are enjoined in this stage. The householder is respected most since he supports the three other stages. In the third stage of *Vanaprastha* the individual is required to check his attachment to worldly possessions, suppress all the conceits bred in him through the accidents of the second stage, such as pride of birth or property, individual genius or good luck, and cultivate a spirit of renunciation. When he is thoroughly disciplined for the higher life he becomes a *sanyasin*, a disinterested servant of humanity who finds his peace in the strength of spirit. A state of perfect harmony with the Eternal is reached, and the education of the human spirit terminates.

These *sanyasis* do not cut themselves off from the world and let it go to rack and ruin. The greatest of their class, Buddha and Sankara, Ramanuja and Ramananda, and scores of others, have entered into the life blood of the nation and laid the foundations of its religion. Their names are to-day a part of the national heritage.

The caste rules relate to the social functions of individuals. Man's nature can be developed only by a concentration of his personality at a particular point in the social order. Since human beings show one or other of the three aspects of mental life in a greater degree, the *dvijas* or the twice-born are distinguished into the three classes, of men of thought, men of feeling, and men of action. Those in whom no one quality is particularly developed are the *Sudras*. These correspond to the intellectual, militant, industrial, and unskilled workers, who are all members of one organic whole. So early as the period of the Rigveda was the organic nature of society brought out by the metaphor of head, arms, trunk and legs, answering to the four classes which are bound by ties of common fellowship. Each class has its appropriate place, rights, and duties in the whole. Since all work is noble, caste pride and exclusiveness are not encouraged. *Caste implies responsibilities and not rights.* No one is free from any quality, though different qualities predominate in different men. The fulfilment of our functions is not merely a contribution to the whole but also a mode of self-expression. The unique nature of each individual realises itself in his work, which in a special sense is his own work, *swadharma.*(14)

The ideal of the Hindu dharma is to make all men Brahmins, all people prophets. Then they gain the inward liberty and the joy of spiritual communion, and spontaneously refrain from resisting evil by force, returning violence for violence, and possess the patience and the love to bear it if any beats them, and yield to his wishes if any would deprive them of anything. They are filled with the spirit of peaceful joy or *sante*, which means the extinction of all hate. The Brahminhood represents the highest of which human nature is capable. The social fabric is organised on the basis of spiritual perfection. Man has no wings to soar to the heights; he has therefore to be content with scaling them through effort and pain, step by step. The Hindu social organisation embodies this graduated scheme. I may illustrate this point by two examples of ahimsa or non-violence and cow-protection. "Thou shalt not slay," neither men nor animals. It is the highest law, the only law worthy of man. Every Brahmin is asked to respect it, yet the system provides for a class of warriors whose profession it is to kill and get killed. The organisers felt that the spirit of retaliation, "an eye for an eye, a tooth for a tooth," was firmly rooted in human nature. It cannot be suddenly displaced. When submission to evil is wrong, when resisting it by love is impossible, then resistance by violence is allowed, and the warrior classes are told that it is their duty to resist aggression by force. It is, however, a concession to human nature, and the Kshatriya is told that the law of love which the Brahmin practises is higher than the law of brute force which he himself employs. The Kshatriya represents a lower stage of development, since he looks upon man as a lump of flesh, and not a spark of God. He is called upon to fight in a spirit of brotherliness, without hate and out of a sense of duty, and not in a vindictive mood - that he who has made me suffer must suffer too. If the Kshatriya acts in this spirit of humanity, he will rise in spiritual status and rely less on brute force, until at last he becomes a Brahmin incapable of injuring any living thing on earth. Though violent resistance is allowed, the end is to transcend it. We have to sail along the current of nature in order to reach beyond it.

The law against killing applies to the animal world also. Its logical implication is that we should abstain from animal food. The animal creation is also from God, and so has to be treated with kindness. The cow is the symbol of the animal world. The daily prayer of the regenerate Hindus asks for the protection of the cow and the Brahmin symbols of the animal and the human worlds, nourishers of our bodies and souls respectively. Gandhi writes: "Why the cow was" selected for apotheosis is obvious to me. The cow was in India man's best companion. She was the giver of plenty. The cow is a poem of pity ... the mother to millions of Indian mankind. Protection of the cow means protection of the whole dumb creation of God."(15) But there were people in India who showed no pity or mercy for the animal world. They had to be trained out of their habits. The ideal of the Brahmin who abstains from all animal food, who hurts no being either for sport or food, has been ennobling in its influence. The warriors and the traders are chiefly vegetarians. Even the Sudras on sacred days abstain from animal food. Thus there is a steady growth towards vegetarianism. Those who have absolutely no scruples about the treatment of animals are the *Panchamas*, on whom the influence of Hinduism has not been perceptible.

The charge that Hinduism has done nothing to unchain the moral and spiritual forces of the lower classes displays a colossal ignorance of the work of Hinduism in India. To-day after so many centuries of Buddhism and Christianity, when a civilised race comes into contact with a backward one, it does not care to understand the mentality of the latter, but practises cruel methods of conquest and subjection, that the backward races, if they are left eyes to weep with, spend laborious days and sleepless nights cursing God because He had allowed these civilisers to get into their lands. The Aryans of India accepted the natives into their fold and helped them to get rid of their habits of dirt and drunkenness, lead clean lives and worship the one living God. When the original inhabitants were found worshipping serpents, the Aryans told them that thee was a geater than the serpent-god, the *Nageswara*, the Lord of Serpents, or Krishna who dances on the head of the serpent Kaliya. They did not expose themselves to the avenging power of facts by hurriedly forcing up society to a higher plane of conduct which could not be reached without an inward call. The work of gradual civilising by means of caste continued till the advent of the Muhammedans. In a large country like India, with no easy means of communication, the work achieved is really great. Mr. James Kennedy wites: "The absorption and assimilation of these aboriginal or foreign masses within the Hindu fold was the task of new Hinduism, a task mainly accomplished between the seventh and eleventh centuries A.D.; and it was so thoroughly done that we now find throughout northern India a Hindu population fairly homogeneous in blood, culture, and religion, and sufficiently marked from the degraded tribes that still haunt the outskirts of civilisation."(16) Outsiders have been steadily flowing into the Hindu fold, and the religion has been able to absorb and inspire heterogeneous peoples with elements of the higher life. But for this civilising work India would have had instead of fifty million untouchables, five times that number. This work has ceased to be effective since the loss of political freedom by the Hindus. It was then that Hindu society became fixed up in a conservatism and left outside its pale a considerable part of the population of India, which has been the field for exploitation by the non-Hindu religions.

Tradition :

All Hindus are expected to accept the Vedas as their highest religious authority. They embody the principles of life and of the universe. The vital parts of the Vedas are the Upanishads, products of a perfectly spontaneous spiritual movement which implicitly superseded the cruder aspects of the Vedas. The subsequent history of the Hindu faith has been a steady building on the foundations truly said in the Upanishads. Though religious thought has traversed many revolutions and made great conquests, the central ideas have continued the same for nearly fifty centuries. Whenever dogmatic developments succeeded in imprisoning the living faith in rigid creeds true prophets of the spirit arose and summoned the people to a spiritual revival. When the movement of the Upanishads became lost in dogmatic controversies, and the fever of dialectical disputation lulled the spirit of religion, Buddha insisted on the simplicity of truth and the majesty of the moral law. Probably in the same period, though in another part of the country, when canonical culture and useless learning made religion inhuman scholasticism, and filled those learned in this difficult trifling with ridiculous pride, the author of the Gita opened the gates of heaven to all those who are pure in heart. Sankara's reformation of the Indian religion is not yet a spent force. Ramanuja and Madhwa, Kabir and Nanak, have left permanent marks on the Hindu faith. It is clear that Hinduism is a process, not a result; a growing tradition, not a fixed revelation. It never shut off by force wisdom from anywhere, for there are no distinctions of mine and thine in the Kingdom of Spirit.

1. Rajogunah, mrito brahma, vishnoh sattvagunatmakah, tamogunah statha rudro, nirgunah parameswarah.
2. cf. Ps. xviii. 25-26
3. "Apsu devamanushyanam, divi manishinam batanam I Kashtaloshteshu, Buddhastvatmani devatah. I Agnou Kriyavato devo, hirdi devo manishinam pratimasvalpabuddinam, Jnaniam sarvatah sivah." See Bhagwan Das : Vaidika Dharma, which has a number of relevant texts.
4. Paramatmanah sarvepi padarthah avirbhavopadhayah.
5. Manu, I
6. Atmanam manusham manye ramam dasarathatmajam. "And call no man your father on the earth : for one is your father, even he who is in heaven." Matthew xxiii; cf. Mark x, 18.
7. On this whole question, see the chapter on the Bhagavadgita in my book on Indian Philisophy, Allen & Unwin.
8. Plato : Timoeus, 29, c.
9. "Sarvastaratu durgani, sarvo bhadrani pasyatu I sarvastad buddhi mapnotu sarvassarvatra nandatu."Bhagavata purana; cf. Spinoza's saying that "the highest good is, common to all and all may equally enjoy it."
10. Uttamasahajavastha, dvitiya dhyanadharana / tritiya pratimepuja homayatra chaturdhika.
11. Pp. 98-99.
12. Sivamatmani pasyanti pratimasu na yoginah.
13. Dharanad dharma mityahu, dharmena vidhrutah prajah.
14. I have not here referred to the bearing of the caste system on village government and trade guilds, or to the present corrupted state of the institution.
15. Young India, 6th October, 1921.
16. Imperial Gazetteer, vol. ii chap viii.

THE HINDU DHARMA

From the time the histroy of the Aryans in India commenced up till to-day, it has been the privilege or the misfortune of India to be faced with serious racial and religious crises. In a special sense, India has been a small edition of the world serviving as a laboratory where experiements of racial and religious syntheses relevant to the problems of the world are undertaken and worked out. If it be true that every people has its own distinctive note and brings out one particular aspect of the divine manifestation, India seems to have been selected, in the economy of things, for the purpose of offering solutions for racial and religious conflicts.

In the long history of the Hindu religion with all its cross currents and backwaters, with the windings of the stream and the barren expanses of sand, it is possible to discern a general tendency, a spiritual direction which has continued the same in spite of varying expressions. The central principles of the ancient Hindu dharma are not dead shells, but living powers full of strength and suggestiveness. Even if it be not so, it is not altogether without interest to understand the principles of the Hindu faith which has more than two hundred million followers to-day.

The term "dharma" is one of complex significance. It stands for all those ideals and purposes, influences and institutions that shape the character of man both as an individual and as a member of society. It is the law of right living, the observance of which secures the double object of happiness on earth and salvation.(1) It is ethics and religion combined. The life of a Hindu is regulated, to a very detailed extent, by the laws of dharma. His fasts and feasts, his social and family ties, his personal habits and tastes are all considered by it.

Moksha or spiritual freedom is the aim of all human life. It is the destiny of man to reach the summits of spirit and attain immortality. We are the children of God, *Amritasya Putrah.* The eternal dream of the human heart, the aspiration of the soul to come to its own is the basis of the Hindu dharma. It assumes that the fundamental reality is the soul of man. All the desires of heart, all discussions of logic pre-suppose the reality of the *Atman.* It is something unprovable by reason, though no proof is possible without it. Nor is it a mere matter of faith, since it is the faith which underlies all reason. If the self of man is open to doubt, thennothing on earth is free from it. If anything can be, then the soul is. It is the ultimate truth which is above all change, the unseen reality which is the basis of all life and logic. It is the mystery which silently affirms itself. What our minds think is not of much importance beside the truth that we are. The fears of man are due to the imperfections which shut him from his destiny, the darkness which hides the light within. If we take refuge in the self, the only fixed point of our being, we shall know that we are not alone in the apparently endless road of life or *samsara* and that we can overcome the world and defy death. "Greater is he that is within you than he that is in the world."(2)

While the spiritual perfection of man is the aim of all endeavour, the Hindu dharma does not insist on any religious belief or form of worship. The utmost lattitude is allowed in the matter of addressing and approaching the supreme. The Hindu thinkers were good students of philosophy and sociology and never felt called upon to enforce religious belief. Misunderstandings and antagonisms in religious matters arise, when we put forward excessive claims on behalf of our own views of God. Besides, religion implies freedom and it is the greatest injury that we can inflict on man to compel him to accept what he cannot understand. Again, it is difficult to classify the ways of man to God. The heart of man has written, in its blood its pathway to God. A Sanskrit verse says, "As the birds float in the air and the fish swim in the sea leaving no traces behind, even so are the paths traversed by the spiritual." Christ spoke of the mystery of the divine life revealing itself in the finite soul. "The wind bloweth where it listeth; thou hearest the sound thereof, and canst not tell whence it cometh or whither it goeth, so is every one that is born of the spirit." God reveals himself now by a flash of lightning, now by a tremor in the soul. To a Hindu who has understood the spirit of his religion all faiths are sacred. In Rabindranath's school at Bolpur, where the one Invisible God is worshipped, abuse of others faiths is disallowed. Gandhi is most tolerant in his religious views. Regarding the attitude of the Brahmin thinkers to other religions, Wilson writes, "The Brahmins who compiled a code of Hindu law, by command of Warren Hastings, preface their performance by affirming the equal merit of every form of religious worship. Contrarieties of belief, and diversities of religion, they say, are in fact part of the scheme of providence; for as a painter gives beauty to a picture by a variety of colours, or as a gardener embellishes his garden with flowers of every hue, so God appointed to every tribe its own religion that man might glorify him in diverse modes, all having the same end and being equally acceptable in his sight."(3)

This does not, however, mean that the Hindu thinkers have no right ideas of God and consider all beliefs to be equally true. They have a sure perception of the highest truth, though they do not insist on a universal acceptance of it. They believe that if the mind is enlightened the truth will be spontaneously perceived. Every religion is an expression of the mental and social evolution of the people who adopt it. It is therefore mischievous to attempt any sudden supplanting of existing beliefs by new ones. The cruder conceptions will give way before the rising rational reflection and the true reformer tries to improve the mental and moral nature of men. Truth is not so much the result of theological faith as the experience of a deeper moral life. So the Hindu thinkers pay more attention to the discipline than to the doctrine. The religion of the Hindus is not a theology as a scheme of life. Whether one is an orthodox Hindu or not depends, not on whether one believes this or that view of God, but on whether one accepts or rejects the *dharma*.. (4)

The highest life enjoined by the dharma is what follows naturally from vital faith in the reality of God. If the indwelling of God in man is the highest truth, conduct which translates it into practice is ideal conduct. The several virtues are forms of the truth, *satyakaras*.(5) Truth, beauty and goodness are a part of the life stuff of the ideal man. He will be an embodiment of the virtues of the self denial, humility, fraternal love and purity. By the mastery of soul over sense, clouds of hate and mists of passion dissolve and he will be filled with *santi* or serenity and will remain absolutely calm in moments of great peril, personal loss or public calamity. With tranquillity of soul, a steady pulse and a clear eye he will do the right thing at the right moment. He does not belong to this country or that, but is in a true sense the citizen of the world. The quality of *sattva* with its ideals of joy and love predominates over those of *rajas* with its craving for power and pride and *tamas*, with its dulness and inertia. For the perfect men, the dharma is an inspiration from within; for others it is an external command, what custom and public opinion demand.

The ideal which requires us to refrain from anger and covetousness, to be pure and loving in thought, word and deed is much to high for those passing through the storm and stress of a life of sin and suffering. It seems to demand of life what is possibly cannot give. It kills all the constituent conditions of life. If renunciation of all were necessary for salvation, many may not care to be saved. The world is so organized that those who practise the Divine rule do not have much chance of success or survival. We are familiar with the way in which the Sermon on the Mount is dismissed as impossible idealism. We cannot be turning cheeks to smiters to receive blows when it is so tempting to give blows on both the cheeks. It may be divine to rejoice in suffering, but the flesh is weak for all that. Christendom consoles itself in the belief that even Jesus nodded once or twice. "O, my Father, if it be possible, let this cup pass from me." "My God, my God, why hast thou forsaken me?" Those who pride themselves on their practical spirit reduce the ideals to the level of ordinary human nature, subject to the temptations of power and profit, the flesh and the devil. The modern wordly reformer says, "Ye have heard that it was said by them of old time, 'Thou shalt not kill, but I say unto you, 'Thou shalt not kill except animals for food, birds for sport and men in battle.' It hath been said, 'Thou shalt not covet.' But I say unto you, 'Thou shalt not covet except on a large scale as in trade and imperialism.' Again, ye have heard that it hath been said by them of old time, 'Thou shalt not hate,' but I say unto you, 'Thou shalt not hate except the backward races, the enemy nations and the weak of the world." Alarmed at the sacrifices exacted by a religious life which tells us that happiness does not depend on power or wealth but on love and peace, our advanced reformers make so many reservations to the divine law that they completely destroy the force of the latter and justify our modern practice that violence, abundance of possessions and armaments are the final end of man's life. They conveniently forget the story of that friend of ours who planned to build great storehouses to provide an abundance for many years but was cheated of his chance by the blow of death, which came overnight.

The Hindu thinkes are conscious of the great gulf that separates the actual nature of man which is bad from the ideal which seems to be well nigh impossible. The consciousness of the great distance between the actual and the ideal does not tempt them to distort the ideal itself. It would be a blasphemy against the spirit in us that shall not be forgiven. They therefore attempt to develop the infinitely precious ideal from out of the apparently refractory stuff of life. The nature of man and his habits of judgement change rather slowly. We must have patience in the striing after perfection. The law of Karma tells us that millions of lives are consumed before one perfect life is produced. For thought to reach the highest plane we must plan, toil and agonize a lot. For our heart to pulse with joy, countless hearts must be burned out by suffering. Many strivings and sacrifices are needed to generate a holy character. Most men climb up the ladder to the spiritual heights only rung by rung. Few can fly from the bottom to the top at one bound. The **varnasrama dharma** or the discipline of the classes and stages of life is the Hindu's device for the gradual improvement of human nature. It is intended to make all the Lord's people prophets. Its principles are those of a kingdom of spirit, not a civil commonwealth, of a universal instituion, not a national organization. If morality is that which conscience imposes, and law that which state commands, the **dharma** is neither the one nor the other. It is the tradition sustained by the conviction of countless generations of men, which help to build the soul of truth in us. It corresponds to the *Sittlichkeit* of the Germans and is independent of both the individual conscience and the laws of the state. That is why dynastic feuds and imperialist aggressions have not touched the life of India which has continued the same for nearly fifty centuries. Successive storms of conquest have passed over the changeless millions as wind over reeds.

Moksha or liberation is the ideal towards which humanity has to move. All life is set to the music of this ideal. All men are equal in that they are born of God. they are equal since they are to rise to the same divine destiny. But men differ with regard to their actual equipment for the ideal. They have varying amounts of darkness and evil to eliminate and have to put forth varying efforts to illumine their life with light and love. The education of the individual spirit is arranged through the scheme of **asramas** or stage of life **varnas** or classes of men. It takes into account the different sides of human nature. The life of man is rooted in desires or *kama*. Man is a bundle of desires. Manu says, 'It is not good that the soul should be enslaved by desire, yet nowhere is to be found desirelessness (akamata).(6) Since our activities are impelled by our desires, the right regulation of our desires is also a part of dharma. So **kama** or enjoyment is recognized as a valid pursuit. It is not mere satisfaction of animal impulses but is the expression of the freedom of the self. This is not possible, until we escape from the tyranny of the senses. The life of man is not a mere succession of sensations but is the manifestation of an eternal idea developing itself through temporay forms. The desires of men are directed into the channels of family life and public duty. The emotional or artistic life of man is also a part of life's integral good. But art cannot flourish in an atmosphere of asceticism. We must have wealth or *artha*. The economic needs of the community should be satisfied, if the creative impulses of men are to be liberated for the higher cultural life. Rules are laid down regarding the interests of the community in the matter of the wealth earned by individual members. The liberty of each is restricted by the needs of all. Self-denial is the only way to gain wealth and enjoyment. **Dharma** or duty controls the pursuit of both pleasure and profit, **kama** and **artha**. Those in whom dharma predominates are of **sattvik** nature, while the seekers of wealth are mere **rajasik** and those of pleasure tamasik.(7) The individual who observes the laws of dharma automatically attains **moksha**, and so is it said that dharma, artha, kama and moksha, form the ends of life.

Whoever may have made the world or not, whatever be the truth about the origin of life and the universe, the supremacy of the moral end is admitted by all. In Hindu thought, man is said to come into being for a divine purpose. The unextinguished passions of our vanished lives bring about our birth on earth. It is through suffering that our weakness can be converted into strength, our ignorance into illumination. The evil of existence is expiated only by the suffering and self-restraint of life. The word *"asrama"* comes from a root which means "to suffer." Without sufferig, there is no progress; without death, no resurrection. Our life from beginning to end is a kind of death which means a larger life. The more we die to ourselves, the more do we live to God. Living and dying are inextricably blended and the perfect life is the crown of a complete death. Four stages are distinguished in the life of every Hindu, of which the first two are those of *Brahmachari* or student, *Grihastha* or householder. The last two stages deal with the retirement from life when the individual becomes a servant of God and of humanity.(8)

The first period opens with the sacramental symbol of initiation into a spiritual birth. It is intended to build up the psychophysical constitution of man. The building of the body and the training of the mind are the principal aims of this stage. The student is taught the habits of cleanliness, chastity, good manners and godliness. (9) Social sympathies are cultivated by the insistence on poverty for all students whether they are sons of princes or of peasants. Every student is required to beg for his food and this training in poverty impresses on the mind of the student that wealth is not an essential condition of a good life. The students are not allowed to become laws unto themselves; nor are they delivered into the hands of an ignorant and blind fanaticism. They are not allowed to build altars and idols in their own imagination or fall a prey to superstitions and creeds. Loyalty to truth and respect for tradition are insisted on. The kind of education depends on the needs and capacities of the boys. The task was not so complex as it is to-day since the future vocations of boys were roughtly settled. In the programme of education, secular as well as religious, no distinction is made between boys and girls. Only co-education was not encouraged.

When the stage of apprenticeship is over, the student becomes responsible for a family: "The man is not man alone, but his wife and children also." (10) He becomes the bread-winner of the family and thus the mainstay of the community. Family life and social duty help towards the ultimate goal and presuppose self-restraint. Every man is expected to do his work for the world. He should not, out of mere selfish pleasure, abstain from social service. (11) We are pledged to one another and should live for one another, the individual for the family, the family for the community, the community for the nation and the nation for the world. The caste system, valid in the second stage of the householder, assumes the unity and the interdependence of humanity. It takes into account the needs of the society as well as the interests of the individual. It sustains personality in that it helps the individual to transcend himself by giving his devotion to something beyond himself. By focusing his energies at a paticular point in the environment, he tries to actualize his potentialities. It is an illustration of Hegel's harmony of opposites, a point of view which reconciles the apparently conflicting claims of the individual and the society. Not the good of self as a thing apart, or the good of society by itself, but a higher good to promote which constant self-renewal and social service are means is the governing principle of the caste system. Taking into account the variety of human nature, it lays down ways and means by which each man can attain full self-expression. It works up to the ideal of equality by recognizing the actual differences. It is an attempt to co-operate with the forces of nature and not flout them. Those who criticize the institution from the platform of modern knowledge do not remember that in no other country were peoples belonging to stocks of very unequal value thrown together.

The pre-vedic peoples with whom the Aryans had to mingle were of a lower grade of civilization and culture. They were constituted into the fourth estate of the unregenerate, the once-born, the **ekajati**, in whom no quality of intellect, emotion, or will is particularly developed. The twice-born or the regenerated are divided into three classes according as their intellect, emotion or will is more dominant than the others. Those who are strongly endowed with the powers of thought and reflection are the **Brahmins**; those gifted with heroism and love are the **Kshatriyas** or the warriors; those stongly inclined towards the practical business of life are the **Vaisyas** or the traders. The four classes correspond to the intellectual, the militant, the industrial and the unskilled workers. All of them serve God's creation, by their own capacities, the **Brahmins** by their spirituality, the **Kshatriyas** by their heroism, the **Vaisyas** by their skill and the **Sudras** by their service.(12) All of them place the common good above that of their party or class. Claims of egoism and ambition are subordinated to those of conscience and justice, the enduring values that are confided to our keeping. When the different classes fulfil their respective functions, the society is considered to be just or in accordance with *dharma*.

The true interests of the unskilled workers were not neglected. The **Vaisyas** pursue trade and love, wealth and comfort though they are required to interpret them in terms of life and welfare. This caste is an association of men united by an economic nexus, Commercialism, however, was checked since the members of this class were called upon to hold the goods of life in the bonds of love. The Kshatriyas were the defenders of society from external aggression and internal disorder. The military organisation of the state was entrusted to them. They were in charge of the political arrangements. It was not the intention of the Hindu dharma to make the body of the people act as a general militia. Efficiency is everywhere gained through specialisation. Those whose business it is to make war and resist wrong by force must possess the proper aptitude for it and get the necessary training. The art of Government cannot be practised by all. It is increasingly felt that amateur politicians keen on satisfying their constituencies and with no other training than what could be got from the hurly-burly of popular elections are incapable of doing justice to the task of administration. One paticular class was devoted to the military and the administrative purposes, and the people as a whole were not possessed by a passion for Government, for domination and power. To-day, the great wars are fought for the Government of the world and for the possession of its markets and not for the moral elevation of the people or the pursuit of good. The political obsession is the cause for the drifting of the world in deep confusion to unseen issues. It may be said that when there is a professional ruling class, there is no guarantee that the rule will be unselfish. the training to which they are subjected is a sufficient security for the right dischage of their functions. Besides, the rulers are not allowed to annul or alter dharma, but are only to administer it. The changes in the dharma are introduced by the **Brahmin** thinkers, who possess no vested interests, but lead a life of spirit in compulsory poverty. They interpret the dharma in cases of doubt and difficulty.

The organisation of the society is essentially aristocratic in the best sense of the term, since only the philosophically minded men with detachment of view lay down the laws. The priests were the lawgivers even among the Jews, the Iranians and the Celts. The qualifications of the true **Brahmis,** wisdom, self-control and disinterestedness, made selfish legislation difficult. The Brahmins engaged in the pursuit of knowledge and the beautifying of life were regarded as superior to the officers and administrators, and were not obliged to do what is congenial to the latter. They were freed from all material cares and subordination in spiritual matters to earthly authorities.(13) The institution recognises that all good reforms start in the mind of one man and at first repel the world at large. Society cannot progress if all forward steps should first obtain the sanction of the majority. Absolute freedom for the creative thinkers is the first condition of culture and progress. Mr. Bertrand Russell, in a brilliant article in the *Century*, observes "without freedom, the man who is ahead of his age is rendered impotent." The considered conviction of one wise man is more worthy than the opinions of a myriad fools, according to Manu.(14)

The moral codes are adapted to the different stages of the unfolding of the life of spirit. The trader hoards up life zealously for material ends; the warrior flings it away for order and organisation and resists evil by the employment of force. The Brahmin lives the life of *ahimsa* or *non-violence* with zeal and determination. His non-violence is not a sign of weakness or cowardice, but the natural expression of spiritual strength and divine love. He has passed through the stage of a warrior and has found it unworthy of a true believer in God. Centuries of hereditary training and the influence of environment have made the

Hindu a mild passive meditative being, a worshipper of the ideal of the Brahmin **sannyasi**. Even to-day he is willing to pay his profound admiration to an emaciated saint like Gandhi.

The existence of orders lower than the Brahmin, the dedication of one class to the business of war, have misled many students of Hinduism into thinking that the Hindu dharma is not based on the principle of non-violence. The simple explanation that we have to pass through the lower stages in order to transcend them is forgotten. The higher we rise, the more austere should our life be. The legend of St. Christopher, who undertook to carry the Christ child on his shoulders across a stream, is applicable to us all. The deeper he entered into the water, the heavier became the burden. By a slow conquest of the passions, by a rising knowledge of the spiritual basis of the world, all men who are born sudras gradually rise in the scale till they became Brahmis. The load becomes heavier the higher we rise, and our strength will have to increase in proportion to the rise in the weight of the load. While the Kshatriya in view of his limitations may employ force, though without hatred and with a clean conscience, the Brahmin should refrain altogether from the use of force and the cherishing of hatred or ill feeling for any.

The relativity of the stages leading up to the absolute ideal may also be illustrated from another case. Modern evolution is confirming the Hindu theory of the continuity of the animal and the human worlds. The Hindu dharma inculcates respect for life and tenderness towards all forms of animal creation. "Thou shalt not kill" applies to the animals as well. It is also believed that animal diet clogs the finer sensibilities of human life. More than what it adds to the physical it takes away from the psychical. Jesus himself is quite clear that even animals are objects of sacredness, and that not a sparow falls to the ground without the notice of God. Yet the peoples of India were accustomed to animal diet, and so regulations were laid down restricting the use of animal diet for the fourth class and prohibiting it as a rule fo the other classes, with the result that the Hindus as a whole are tending to give it up more.

Caste has economic implications. Many of the modern castes are only occupational divisions. Every man is not fit for all things and does not feel that he can begin any trade as he pleases. Nor do individuals go about in search of work, but they serve society by filling the station in which they happen to be placed. Unlimited competition and selfish individualism are checked. A religious character is impressed on every kind of work and form of industry. The bricklayer and the carpenter, the blacksmith and the milkman believe that they glorify God by right performance of their work. In these days of large-scale production and factory labour, we tend to forget that when a man is cut off from his family and made to work in a large factory, the work becomes joyless and mechanical. The caste on the other hand puts all men working the same profession in their natural surroundings, instead of tearing them away from their homes and working them for long hours and small wages. The fulness of communal life with its living associations of beauty, love and social obligations helps to make the worker happy. The members of his family who share in his work introduce sweetness and humanity into it. If women and children are to be worked, it is better that they work in the atmosphere of a home where it is possible to embody their creative impulses in what they turn out. There is a finer stimulus to right action than mere success in competition or satisfaction of customers can supply. Those who practice the same craft develop coporate feeling and professional honour. The young acquire from the plastic influences of the environment the right kind of vocational training. They absorb unconsciously the tradition of the trade and the economic pursuit happens to be the free self-expression of their soul. It is true that modern conditios are working against cottage industries and small-scale production. But it is not everywhere the case. Fine arts, decorative industries, even spinning and weaving as supplementary interests of the agriculturists may be confined to homes and we can have small factories worked by electricity or oil engines. Caste as trade guilds is not yet out of date. While the suggestion of a definite programme of life at the very beginning is not undesirable, still its stereotyping without the least regard to the natural endowment and special aptitudes is likely to result in an enslavement of life which finds it difficult to adjust itself to the complex condition of the modern world.

Strictly speaking, the caste of a man is determined by the predominance of reason, emotion or will in him which correspond roughtly to the three **gunas** or qualities of *sattva, rajas and tamas.*(15) Manu mentions three principles as governing the caste of a man which are *tapas* or individual effort, *srutam* or the cultural environment and *yoni* or heredity. The first is a vague test and is not available for objective use. The second depends on the home influences, which in their turn depend on the third consideration of birth. The only practicable test is birth, and this view is in consonance with the principles of rebirth and Karma accepted by the Hindus. "The soul that rises with our life's star hath had elsewhere its setting and cometh from afar." Peoples with different racial heritages can live together in amity and fellowship only on the basis of caste. The formulators of the institution felt that though birth was the only available test, spiritual character was the real basis of the divisions of the society. Manu allows that if an individual practices the ways of the good and leads a pure life, he overcomes the effects of heredity.(16) According to the Mahabharata, the test of regeneracy is "not birth, not learning, but only conduct."(17) We hae ignored all factors other than birth, with the result that the system has rigidly confined people for all time to particular compartments, enslaved successive generations of men and proved well nigh fatal to the free growth of social polity. The natural plasticity and fluidity of life are not taken into account by the unflexible moulds and barriers of the system. We have reached a condition of society where the disorganisation of social life is so great that the principle of birth should be subordinated. Referring to a similar state of affairs, the Mahabharata says, "There has been so much mixture in marriages that the test of *jati* or birth is no good. The governing consideration should be *sila* or conduct, and the first Manu has declared that there is no point in distinctions of caste, if character is not considered."(18)

Since the distinction of functions among the different classes is likely to generate pride and exclusiveness, in spite of the training during the student period, the general laws of the equal treatment of all are insisted on. Highest virtue consists in doing to others as we would be done by. *Vishnu Purana* says, "Everywhere ye should perceive the equal; for the realisation of equality or *samatava* is the worship of God."(19) There are duties which men of all caste are required to obey, such as non-injury to life, truth, integrity, cleanliness and self-control.(20) After all, the caste divisions are incidental to our imperfections and should not therefore constitute a source of pride. The one Eternal has no caste. The rules of caste are applicable only in the stage of the householder. Even here, they are not superior to the claims of humanity. What is necessary at the present day is an acceptance of the aims of caste and the cultivation of a more truly social spirit. The blighting bigotries and the rigid restrictions about the amenities of life are inconsistent with humanity and fellowship and therefore are to be given up. Manu does not encourage them. "The ploughman, the friend of family, the cowherd, the servant, the barber and the poor stranger offering his service from the hands of such sudras may food be taken."(21)

The caste rules were not rigid until the advent of the Mohammedans to India. The social laws were fluid and elastic and the mutability of growth was not sacrificed to the strait waistcoat of a legal formula. We read in the Puranas stories of individuals and of families who changed from lower to higher castes. Manu admits the possibility of ascent and decent.(22) Rules for change of caste by gradual purification are also mentioned.(23) The higher strata were accessible to merit from below. When Hindu India lost political freedom and the new rulers adopted a policy of proselytism, social initiative disappeared and law and custom became fetishes, with disastrous results for national solidaity. We have to recover the original spirit of the *dharma*, which was not limited to particular forms, but manifested itself in fresh ones, changing the old and developing the new. The exaggeated value given to caste in times of political insecurity is no more necessary. Caste has a future only if it is confined to social matters. In every society, people enter into marriage relations only with those who are near to them in habits of mind and action. Since a common cultural tradition is better developed among those who pursue the same vocation, marriages among members of the same profession become the order of the day. Even in ancient India, intermariages among members of different castes were not forbidden, though they were not encouraged. *Anuloma* and *Pratiloma* marriages are not usual, though they are not invalid according to Hindu law.(24) If such marriages are not common, it is because they tend to disturb the intimate industrial, social and spiritual life of the community. Caste as a basis of intimate social relations does not interfere with the large life of the nation. As the emperor Ashoka said to his Hindu minister, "Caste may be considered when it is a question of mariage or invitation, but not of the dharma; for the dharma is concerned with virtues and virtues have nothing to do with caste."(25)

It is a bold affirmation of an untruth to argue that social service is unknown to the Hindus. Much capital is made out of the treatment of the untouchables. It is not remembered that a free India rendered them much greater service than what other free countries even in recent times have done for their backward classes. How have the superior nations civilized the Tasmanian and the Australian aborigines, certain Maori peoples and North American Indian tribes ? We generally refine them into extinction and where that is not possible, we sink them into the slough of vice and crime worse than any normal expressions of savage life. If the Kaffir has multiplied under the British protection and the Javanese under the Dutch, if the populations of Straits Settlements and British India have not vanished before their civilizers, it is because a good God has put in a climate unfavourable to the civilizers.

The tropics can never become their habitat. They can be held but not peopled by the Europeans. But for the limits set by nature, the history of the tropical regions would have been different. From the time the Aryans met the peoples of a lower grade of civilization, they devised ways and means by which the different portions of the population could develop in social, spiritual directions. The Aryans even accepted a non-Aryan representative of the "black" peoples and made him deliver the message of the fatherhood of God and the brotherhood of man. Krishna's conduct scandalised society and provoked the Vedic gods of Indra and Brahma. To-day the Aryan worshippers of these gods look upon Krishna as an avatar of God. Krishna, however, had great respect for the Aryan thinkers, and it is said that he washed the feet of the Brahmin guests at the *Rajasuyayagna* of king Yudhisthira. The Aryans took to the non-Aryan gods very kindly, improved them where possible, subordinated them where necessary. The worshippers of Mahisha (buffalo-demon) were told that the Cosmic Spirit was greater than the Mahisha. The worshippers of serpents were instructed that there was a greater than the serpents, the Lord of serpents, Nageswara or Krishna, who danced over the head of Kaliya. The marks of the gradual civilizing of the lower classes are visible throughout the cultural history of India. Whenever there was a tendency to overlook the common humanity of men, a Buddha or a Sankara arose, emphasising the common doom of all high and low. The extent of the country 2,000 miles long and 1,500 miles broad is not similar to that from Dan to Beersheeba. The means of communication that we have at the present day were not available till recently. If the work of civilizing the backward classes had not been undertaken and carried on with zeal and success by the ancient Indians, we would have had not merely fifty millions of these "depressed" classes, but a much larger number. When the outside invaders came into the country, the Hindu felt nervous and as a sheer act of self-preservation stereotyped the existing divisions, and some were left outside the pale of the caste order. Though Manu says that "there is no fifth class anywhere,"(26) the tribes who were not influenced by the dharma formed themselves into the fiftth class. "He who has abandoned his duties is cruel and pitiless, and oppresses others who is passionate and full of destructiveness is a *mleccha*."(27) No words are too strong for the deplorable condition of these people. To disregard the claims of man simply because he happens to be low or belongs to another race is against the religious spirit of Hinduism. Now that things are in a more settled condition, the Hindu leaders are reiterating the central truth that the least of all men has a soul and need not be considered past all power to save.

The last two stages of *Vanaprastha* and *Sannyasa*, which may be taken as one for our purposes, treat of those who have retired from the competitive struggle for life. The *Sannyasi* represents the highest type of Indian manhood. From selfishness, the individual has progressed to self-annihilation through the extinction of all prejudice, hatred and ambition. He has passed through all institutions and is now above them. His emotional life expresses itself in the love of the divine or *bhakti* and not in animal lusts or personal likes. He perceives the oneness and wholeness of humanity, and his mind is freed from all supersition and unreason. His active energies are devoted to the service of humanity, knowing as he does that God is in all beings and is all of them.(28) He who has the vision of all in one, in whom the impersonal predominates over the personal, cannot sin.(29) He is the superman of the

Bhagavadgita, the awakened of Buddhism, the true Brahmin who glories in his poverty, rejoices in suffering, and is finely balanced in mind, with peace and joy at heart. He loves all men, birds and beasts, and resists not evil but overcomes it by love. In him the soul of man is at its highest stretch. The ideal of the *Sannyasi* has dominated the life of India from the time of the Rishis of the Upanishads. To follow this ideal, kings lay down their crowns and sceptres and assume the garb of poverty, fighting heroes forget the pride of victory and break their weapons, and skilled traders and workmen pursue their toil with steadfast mind surrendering to God the fruits thereof.

These *Sannyasis* as a rule are the helpers of humanity. The greatest of them, like Sankara and Ramanuja, Ramananda and Kabir, have entered into the lifeblood of the nation and laid the foundations of its religion. It is, however, true, that in India, as in Mediaeval Europe, many ascetics made the mistake of escaping into the wilderness from the worries of the world. These hermits of the cloister and monks of the desert are voices astray in the dark. Their perpetual consciousness of incitement to sin, their pre-occupation with their selfish salvation show that they have lost their lives in their anxiety to save them. As the tide of monasticism which swept over Europe in the Middle Ages is not true to the teaching of Jesus, who asks us to look upon ourselves as servants trusted by the master, porters bidden to watch, stewards to whom much is committed, sons to whom the father confides his affairs, so the deserters from the battle of life are not the true *Sannyasis* who rage to suffer for mankind, with intense humility, glowing faith, sincere love and sober joy.

To reach the highest state, it is not always necessary to adhere literally to the rules *of dharma*. There are cases of sudden conversion, uprushes of the spirit from seemingly common place souls, astonishing moral elevations among men who have not learned the highest lesson of existence. The rules of *dharma*, however, represent the normal growth of spirit. The freed souls sometimes smile at the irrelevance of the painful scrupulosities and anxious questionings about ceremonial propriety which worry those in the lower stages of life. The order of **Sannyasis** is open to men of all castes. No man, however, should desire liberation without paying his three debts,(30) to the gods by means of hymns and prayers, to the *pitrus* or the fathers by gifts and charity, help and service to men and rearing up of progeny, and to the Rishis by passing on to others the instruction received by himself.

The Hindu Dharma has room for all kinds of men, the dispassionate old who have retired from the business of life and the eager pushful young keen on worldly success. The four castes and orders are not intended to be special moulds into which the Indian people are thrown, but forms capable of embracing the whole of humanity. Without the employment of force or eagerness for exploitation. Hinduism has been able to civilize a lage part of Asia. What has attracted it is not imperialist expansion, but the cultural conquest, the peaceful penetration of the thought and mind of the peoples of which it comes by its own spirituality. From the kingdom of Khotan in Central Asia to the Island of Java, which lies on the way between India and Australia the creative urge of the Hindu genius found its expression in life and art. Java had Hindu settlers in as far back as the second century A.D. and she has remained since then predominantly Hindu and Buddhist. To-day, Japan, China and Burma look to India as their spiritual home even as Christians look to Palestine. Wherever we go from Russia to China, at Samarkand, at Tibet, we can trace the influence of the Indian civilization. All these pale into insignificance when we remember that there are records of Indian culture in Western Asia, in the plains of Mesopotamia, in the regions watered by the rivers Tigris and Euphrates. Inscribed tablets discovered at Boghazkoi, assigned by competent scholars to 1400 B.C., speak to us of people who were worshipping the Hindu gods. This influence of India is not because her religion is old or her empires are great, not because she developed weapons of destruction or exercised force on a large scale, but because she had an intelligent understanding of the deeper unity in the midst of all diversity. Wherever she went, the deep and silent influence of her vision of the unity of all things in God pervaded. All the mighty impulses that entered into India were synthesized on the same plan. All religions she welcomes since she realized from the cloudy heights of contemplation that the spiritual landscape at the hilltop is the same though the pathways from the valley are different. To those who were wandering at random in the plains without suspecting that all roads lead to the same top, she says: Raise your eyes. Things in the valley separate us. Up yonder, high above us, we are all one. The variety of ways has meaning at the foot of the hill, but if we understand what they signify on the snowy summits, we shall know that all are reaching out for God. It may be that India with her assimilative genius may yet succeed in harmonising the mighty currents of the world's great religions that have met on her soil.

1. Abhyudaya and Nihsreyasa.
2. I, John, V, 21.
3. H. H. Wilson : Essays and Lectures, Vol. II, p. 8.
4. See Manu II, 11.
5. See Mahabharata. Anusasana parva 162 and Santi parva 33.
6. II, 2 3.
7. Manu. XII, 38.
8. Manu VI, 87.
9. Manu II, 69.
10. Manu IX, 45
11. The Bhagavadgita III, 16.
12. Sukraniti I, 38-42.
13. Manu IV, 11.
14. XII, 113.
15. See Bhavishya purana III, IV, 23.
16. See also Mahabharata. Vanaparva, Ch. 216.
17. Vrittam eva, M. B. Vanaparva Ch. 314.
18. Vanaparva, Ch. 182. See Manu IV, 224 and 225.
19. XVII.
20. Manu X 63; VI, 91-92.
21. Manu IV, 253.
22. See X, 42; IX, 335.
23. Manu X, 57-65.
24. See Bombay Law Reporter. Bai Gulab vs. Jivanlal Hiralal Vol. XXIV.
25. Indian Social Reformer, June 4, 1922.
26. X, 4.
27. Sukraniti I. 44.
28. Sarva Bhutamayam harim. Vishnu Purana I, 19, 9.
29. Manu XII, 118.
30. See Manu VI, 35.

ISLAM & INDIAN THOUGHT

I

We find at the present day an eager quest in many directions after a higher wisdom, a more adequate philosophy of life than satisfied our fathers. Traditional bonds of religious opinion are loosened hardly ever before and men claim absolute freedom as to think as they like and mould their theories of life anew under the impulses of the hour. Novelties of thought seem to have a greater fascination for our modernist minds than the results of ancient wisdom and modesties of ancient reverence.. The present unsettlement is a challenge to the ancient creeds to revindicate their validity and usefulness. The spiritual leaders of all progressive religions are now busy, rethinking their traditional views so as to rescue them from the assaults of advancing knowledge and experience. In the book under review Sir Ahmed Hussain, a distinguished Indian Moslem of broad culture and religious seriousness, attempts to indicate the lines along which the religion of Islam be interpreted if it is not to conflict with modern ideals of science and philosophy. We get from it an idea of the kind of contribution which India is likely to make to the future reconstruction of Islam.

The development which a religion assumes in any country depends upon its cultural tradition and national character. In Arabia, Islam was a simple lofty theism, quite a stranger to the refinements of the later centuries. When it subdued the Persian people, the semitic tendencies yielded to the mystic ones. The incomparable beauty of the primitive Arab tradition gave place to rich philosophy and gorgeous mythlogy in which Mohammad became a mysterious being suspended between heaven and earth. About 70 millions of the population of India are followers of Islam and the vast majority of them are ethnologically of the same type as the Hindus. It is but natural that the Indian form of Islam should have its own features. Till the other day, the Indian Moslem felt it to be his proud privilege to bring to bear on the interpretation of Islam his own spiritual heritage. Latterly however, a curious notion has got hold of some of our, strange to say, educated Mohammadan brethren, that by transferring their allegiance to the faith of Islam, they became the descendants of the Moors of Spain and the Caliphs of Baghdad. They regarded themselves as culturally and socially distinct from their Hindu fellow countrymen. We do not change our whole mental makeup, simply because we change our intellectual beliefs or religious convictions. To change one's creed is not to cut oneself off from the past of one's country or its ideals, It is a welcome sign of the times that the Indian leaders of Moslem thought and practice are realising the common spiritual heritage of India and protesting against the artificial cleavages which false prophets and designing politicians have encouraged. Whatever our faiths be, the same blood runs in our veins and we are all heirs of a great spiritual inheritance. What A.E. says of Ireland is truer of India. "We are among the few races still remaining on earth whose traditions run back to the gods and the divine origin of things."(2) The fact of India reaches back into the mists of antiquity and so many traditions, appeal to us, even against our will sometimes, touch hidden chords, stir the memory and open the forgetful eyes. The spirit of India is the *elan vital*, the brooding over-soul which makes us all Indians. With a spacious spiritual background, it is the privilege of the Indian Moslem to interpret the faith of Islam, in its truest, highest and noblest sense so as to distinguish it from the creed professed to-day by the ignorant bigot, the political intriguer and the religous fanatic. If the Indian Moslem combines his inherited tradition with his acquired faith and effects a synthesis of the old and the new, he will be led to emphasize those neglected aspects of the truth of Islam which really promoted culture and civilisation and brought to life a dying world and discard those unimportant details which happened to be exaggerated out of all proportion on account of historical accidents. He will break the yoke of the crystallised religion which pervades and blindly influences the life of the people and give the world of Islam an interpretation of the message of Mohammad, which, I venture to say, will be more in accord with the spirit of the prophet than with the dogmatic developments of his later followers. The Hon'ble Mr. Amir Ali in his great book on "The Spirit of Islam" (on which I have drawn freely in this paper) and Sir Ahmed Hussain in his "Notes on Islam" give us a foretaste of the wonderful flowers which will grow out of the seedbed of India's past.

II

What appeals to the Indian imagination in the life of Mohammad is his deeply religious nature. Trying to peep into the mysteries of creation, Mahommad used to take himself for prayer and meditation to a cave on Mount Hira and there he used to remain whole nights plunged in deep thought and meditation. With him, religion was an effort to know the truth and live it. By interpreting religion as life, we adopt a sane attitude to creeds and traditions. Creeds are true only to the extent that they correspond to the knowledge of the facts of life. Experience is not merely the fulfilment but also the test of creeds and every age is called upon to reinterpret the creeds in the light of growing experience. The restatement of the principles of Islam given by Sir Ahmed Hussain is naturally neither quite orthodox, nor quite hererodox, but something midway between the two (p 7). Our author is not prepared to swear by the literal interpretations of the words of the Qu'ran as given by the church doctors but feels free to interpret them as seems most reasonable to him. In doing so he is true to the spirit of Mohammad who lays down no restrictions likely to keep enchained the consience of advancing humanity. Revelation of God is only through the human soul and we are not compelled to believe that the wisest of those to whom they were made were free from the errors and prejudices of the age in which they lived. In the Qu'ran there are ever so many things, of strictly local and temporary interest, which are not at all relevant to religion *qua* religion. The conservatives of all creeds forget that "the dry bones of a religion are nothing, the spirit that quickens the bones is all" (p 12). Sir Ahmed Hussain distinguished Islam from the dogmatic Mohammedanism of some of our moulvies, "I make a difference between Islam and Mohammadanism. The latter is not pure Islam. It has forgotten the spirit of Islam and remembers only the letter of its law" (p 12 note a).

When we take our stand on the 'experience' side of religion, we realise that the truly religious men of all faiths are nearer each other than they imagine. In the broad spirit of Hinduism, our author recognises that the truth intended by all religions is the same and quotes with approval Zalalud-din Rumi's saying, "All religions are in substance one and the same.(3) It is impossible for the Indian Moslem to accept wholeheartedly the spirit of exclusiveness which is a marked feature of semitic religions. India has stood for religious freedom and harmony from the beginning of her history. In accord with this spirit, the great Akbar tried to fuse all Indians into a homogeneous nation by the unifying bond of a common religion int he practice of which both Mohammadans and Hindus would join hands, though he failed in his attempt as the conditions were not in his favour. Considerably influenced by the idealism of the Upanishads, which steer clear of all images and dogmas and thus have universal value, Dara Shukoh, the great grandson of Akbar, wrote a work on *Majmaya Bahrain* or the union of the two oceans (of Hinduism and Islam). He recognised that the two religions were equally efficient in helping us to live higher life. Sir Ahmed Hussain holds that through different angles of approach, we may reach the same goal of salvation. "Please remember that there are many men and many minds and there are likely to be as many religions, as many conceptions of God, as many notions of His attributes and as many ideas of the beginning or end of things as there are thinking minds." (p 24). For those who are familiar with the practice of the mass of Mohammadans, it may perhaps be difficult to believe that this catholic view represents the teaching of the Qu'ran. It is, however, nothing more than the truth. The erroneous belief that there is no true religion besides Islam breeds bigotry, intolerance and fanaticism and is contrary to the teachings of the Qu'ran. "The first verse of the second sura commands us to believe in not only what was revealed to Mahommad but also in what was revealed to those who went before him. It clearly indicates that there are and will ever be, many true religions of which Islam is one." (See page 65.(4)

The religious genius of Mohammad is evident from the fact that he imposed no credal tests. "Whoever says 'there is no God but God' will attain salvation" is almost the first saying of Mohammad reported in the collections of his traditions. Mohammad protests against the exclusiveness of the Jewish and the Christian creeds and declares that all those who believe in God and do His will are eligible for salvation. "They say, verily, none shall enter Paradise except those who are Jews or Christians...say, Produce your proof, if Ye speak the truth nay, but he who directeth towards God and doth that which is right he shall have his reward with his Lord" (Sura V. 105-6). "Verily, those who believe (the Moslems) and those who are Jews, Christians or Sabaeans, whoever hath faith in God and the last day, and worketh that which is right and good for them shall be the reward with their Lord; there will come no fear on them; neither shall they be grieved. (Sura V. 69). With true insight, Mohammad lays stress on conduct more than on doctrine. Every religion which promotes goodness is worthy of acceptance whatever be its dogmatic details, for if we do the will, we shall know the doctrine. "To every one have we given a law and a way. And if God had pleased, He would have made you all one people (professing one religion). But He hath done otherwise that He might try you in that which He hath severally given unto you; wherefore press forward in good works. Unto God shall Ye return and He will tell you that concerning which Ye disagree" (Sura V. 48(5)). According to the Qu'ran Moslems are "those who believe and work righteousness," all those "who trust in the Lord and do good"(6) In conformity with this view, H.H. The Aga Khan said the other day that Mahatma Gandhi was a Moslem. Even Jesus did not say "By their beliefs Ye shall know them" but he said, "By their fruits Ye shall know them" and Peter rightly observes: "Of a truth I perceive that God is no respecter of persons; but in every nation he that feareth Him and worketh righteousness is accepted with Him."(7)

Sir Ahmed Hussain is not wrong when he says that Islam "is not inconsistent with true Christianity or any other *true* religion" (p 12) for all religions have for their essence the fatherhood of God and the brotherhood of man. Only the sectarian dogmatic creeds fight one another. The faith of Jesus as akin to the faith of Mohammad. But when St. Paul asks us to believe in Jesus as our saviour, the very God descended into humanity, a proposition which thinking christians find it increasingly difficult to defend Christianity becomes opposed to Islam which is naturally tempted to put forward equal claims for Mohammad. To the credit of Islam, it must be said that its view of Mohammad is a reasonable one. It regards him as a prophet or a messenger of God who reformed the religion of a considerable part of mankind. For all that, he was only a man like any other mortal, subject to sin and having need as other men, of the mercy of God. "It is not Islam or Eman to defy Mohammad or to represent him to be akin to God, as sometimes some moulvies represent him and call him the one (Ahad) in the guise of Ahmad. "Our prophet himself never claimed that he was anything more than a mere man" (p 37). "God has not sent me" says Mohammad, "to work wonders. he has sent me to preach to you. I never said that Allah's treasures are in my hand, that I knew the hidden things or that I was an angel...I who cannot even help or trust myself unless God pleaseth" (Sura XVII, 95-98; LXXII, 21-24). Yet the devotion and enthusiasm of his first followers were so great that legends arose round the figure of Mohammad. On the night the Prophet was born, it is said, the palace of Chosroes was thrown down by an eathquake, the sacred fire of the Magi was extinguished, the lake of Sawa was died up, the Tigris overflowed, and all the idols of the world fell with their faces to the ground. These traditions, fortunately, never became consecrated legends. Thanks to the scepticism and incredulity of his early Arab followers, even the stories about Mohammad's nocturnal journey to Jerusalem and the voice of God hailing him as His apostle in his wanderings near Mecca, never became so essential to the religion of Islam, as say, those of Ascension and Resurrection to the religion of Christianity. Even the Messiahship of the prophet is not always reverenced. Witness the movement of the Wahabis, who proclaim that worship of God consists in prostrating oneself before Him that the invocation of an intercessor near him is an act of idolatry and that the most meritorious work would be to raze the tomb of the prophet and the mausoleums of the Imams !

It is impossible for a thinker like Mohammad to advocate forced conversions. We cannot compel men to change their beliefs. "Let there be no compulsion in religion" (Sura II 257). "Wilt thou then force men to believe, when belief can come only from God ?"(8) It is doubtful whether Mohammad had any idea of the conversion of non-Arabs to Islam. Religious persecutions and forced conversions which have soiled the fair name of Islam are repugnant to its true spirit. Omar, the persecutor of Islam who later became its apostle, first drew the sword against those who did not blindly admit the beliefs of Islam and the crude practices of some of Muhammad's followers led to the popular view that those who die fighting for their religious beliefs are the truer martyrs. The Indian Moslem shares with his Hindu brother, faith in the freedom of conscience. Sir Abdur Rahim said the other day, "It is a wholly false notion that the religion and law of Islam rejoin conversion by force." (9) The Khilafat movement, whatever be its political value, has certainly helped the cause of religious freedom. Sir Charles Townshend, the defender of Kut-el-Amara wrote recently: "The Hindu population of India has made the cause of religious freedom of all the races of India its own.(10) The spirit of India is teaching Islam to relax some of its severer aspects. Through the interaction of Islam and Hinduism which are to-day looking towards each other, India's vision of harmonising the different religious systems that have met on her soil will be promoted.

III

We may now turn to the doctrinal aspect of Islam and inquire whether its conception of God is radically opposed to the Hindu view. While all religions agree about the objective reality of God, the character of the God worshipped is supposed to give distinction to each religion. According to the Hindu view, no ideas can bring out the mystery of God. God cannot be defined through logical symbols but can be realised in the depths of the soul. If a definition is demanded, we cannot help using the resources at our disposal. We are familiar with our own consciousness and so interpret the nature of God on its analogy. God becomes the divine personality possessing the three characteristics of truth, love and perfection, or wisdom, beauty and power, or infinitude, grace and sovereignty, answering to the three aspects of our conscious life, cognition, emotion and will. The Hindu conception of Trimurti is intended to bring out this threefold nature of Godhead. God as Brahma creates, as Vishnu redeems and as Siva judges. Brahma creates things to suit His ideal forms. His infinite understanding is reflected in the infinite world which was, is and will be. Vishnu is the principle of love at the heart of the infinite power and universal rule. He helps us in our wrestlings with evil and gives a push to the upward ascent. Siva is the judge, the infinite power, "able to do anything, or leave it undone or do in another manner than that in which it is actually done."(11) Whatever name he may give to his God the Hindu has in view this unity of light, love and life. Sir Ahmed Hussain believes that all religions profess belief in one and the same reality, "one and only one God who is Infinite and Absolute, who hath neither beginning nor end, and who is not conditioned or limited by anything whatever. Yezdan, Isvara, Jehovah, God, Allah are the names in different languages of the same Infinite and Absolute God."

The absolute character of God and its incomprehensibility by the finite mind are brought out in many passages of the Qu'ran. The very first verse says: *"Say, He alone is God; God the Eternal. He begetteth not and is not begotten; there is none like unto Him"* While everything else in the world is liable to change and extinction, God alone is. He is the rock in the maelstrom of events in space and time on which we can take our stand, the only hope with which we can face the darkness of the world, its sins and iniquities and yet nothing in the world of space and time is an adequate symbol of the wealth of God. "Sight perceives Him not, but He perceives men's sights; for He is the knower of secrets, the Aware." (Sura VI 104). Caliph Ali condemns all anthropomorphic conceptions of God. "God as not like any object that the human mind can conceive, no attribute can be ascribed to Him which bore the least resemblance to any quality of which human beings have perception from their knowledge of material objects. The perfection of piety consists in *knowing* God; the perfection of knowledge is the affirmation of His verity : the perfection of verity is to acknowledge His unity in all sincerity; and the perfection of sincerity is to deny all attributes to the Deity. God has no relation to place, time or measure,"(12) Man cannot be content with this negative ideal and so he insists on looking upon God as a person. The opening verse of the Qu'ran says "Praise be to God, Nourisher of the words, the Compassionate, the Merciful and King of the day of reckoning" while Vaishnavism and Christianity lay the greatest stress on God as love, Judaism and Islam exaggerate the aspect of God as power. God is Omnipotent Energy and the Eternal Judge. Mohammad frequently speaks of the day of reckoning, when the deeds done by man shall be weighed by the Eternal Judge, when heaven and earth shall be folded up and none be near but God. The other aspects are not however neglected. God is not merely the Judge but also "the forgiver of sin, receiver of penitence" (Sura XL 1-2), the guide of the erring, the deliverer from every affliction, the friend of the bereaved, the consoler of the afflicted, whose love "is more tender than that of the motherbird for her young."(13) Passages emphasising the love of God frequently occur. "Have mercy, O Lord, for of the merciful Thou art the best" (Sura XXII 118). "Is not He the more worthy who answereth the oppressed when they cry to Him and taketh off their ills, and maketh you to succeed your sires on the earth?" (Sura XXVII 62). Seek pardon of your Lord and be turned unto Him; verily my Lord is merciful, loving" (Sura XI 90). "Say O my servants, who have transgressed to your own injury, despair not of God's mercy, for all sins doth God forgive. Gracious, merciful is He" (Sura XXXIX 53). The very name Ar-Rahman with which each chapter opens expresses the conviction that divine love enfolds all creation. It works in man so as to remove the veil from the heart of the creature and draw Him near to God. God is also the creator and nourisher of the world. He is not so much a cold distant deity separated from the World as the Indwelling Presence in nature and history. "God is in the East and the West. Therefore whichever side you turn, you will see the face of God" (I-115) "And He is within you. Why do you not see Him ?" (LI 21). "We will soon show them our sight in all horizons and in their own souls, until it shall become quite clear to them that it is the truth." (XII 53). The three attributes of creation redemption, judgement are assigned to God and the emphasis on Divine unity saves us from tritheism.

The individual soul is made by God and it has no rest until it returns to God. Its complex nature should be made an offering to God. We must use our intellect so as to recognise the presence of God in all things. Belief in the existence of the Supreme naturally produces the sense of entire dependence on God. We pray to God and express in meek humility our thankfulness to Him. The central theme of all prayers is self-humiliation, glorification of the giver of all good and reliance of His mercy. We pour out our grateful hearts through prayers which can be offered anywhere on God's earth. We seek His guidance in daily life and struggle to live up to His ideal. Whether we begin with a logical search for reality (*jnana*) or prayerful devotion to God (*bhakti*) or submission to His laws the end is the same.

The ethics of Islam is of an exalted character. If we are to be worthy of our Father in heaven, we should do nothing which denies the divine origin of man. To develop the truly religious spirit, Mohammad enjoins the observance of prayer, fasting, alms giving and pilgrimages and practice of self-denial. Universal charity is insisted on. Hospitality becomes a religious duty. Chastity is recognised as a virtue. Drunkennes, gambling and other excesses are condemned. Moral life constitutes the essence of piety. "Those who abstain from vanities and the indulgence of their passions, give alms, offer prayers, and tend well their trusts and their covenants, these shall be the heirs of eternal happiness" (Sura XXIII 8). Every Moslem who clothes the naked will be clothed by God in the green robes of Paradise."(14) ***Ibrahim Ben Adhem's*** story which is the basis of Leigh Hunt's well known poem ***Abou ben Adhem*** points the moral that the friend of man is the friend of God. Whatever the actual practice of the mass of Mohammadans may be the religion of Islam is not indifferent to animal life but insists on its sacredness. "There is no beast on earth, nor bird which flieth with its wings, but the same is a people like unto you - unto the Lord shall they return.(15) In the matter of animal sacrifices, the Indian Moslem should remember the significant verse of the Qu'ran. "It is not the flesh or the blood of that which Ye sacrifice which is acceptable to God; it is your piety which is acceptable to the Lord." (Sura XXII 37). Forgiveness and non-resistance are not supposed to be a part of the religion of Islam. It is worth while, in this connection, meditating on the spirit of the following passages : "Turn away evil with that which is better." (Sura XLI 34). Speaking of paradise Mohammad says, "It is prepared for the goodly who give alms in prosperity and adversity, who bridle their anger and forgive men; for God loveth the beneficent" (Sura XLII 7). The many minor details about food, divorce etc. are not directly connected with the religion of Islam. Though Mohammad laid down certain injunctions about them, having in view the circumstances of his time, there is nothing sacrosanct about them. As the Hon'ble Mr. Amir Ali puts it, "with regard to the sumptuary regulations, precepts and prohibitions of Mohammad, it must be remembered that they were called forth by the temporary circumstances of the times and people. With the disappearance of such circumstances, the need for these laws has also disappeared. To suppose therefore that every Islamic precept is necessarily immutable is to do an injustice to history and the development of the human intellect." The Prophet did not inculcate the subjection of human reason to blind authority. A religion which is so strictly limited by commonsense on all sides cannot be made to support inhuman practices to-day. It is for the leaders of Indian Moslem opinion to decide in what details the actual practices of the Indian Moslems require modification if they should live up to the ideal of loving one another, bearing injustice without rebellion, doing harm to none and devoting oneself to universal peace and goodwill.

Those who do not deny the injunctions of the Qu'ran will have a terrible time of it on the day of judgement while those who conform to them will return unto their Lord, their source and support. The ascension of Mohammad is symbolic of the union of the finite and the infinite. Sufism makes out that the end of human development is oneness with God, for he who beholdeth God is Godlike. Jalal-ud-din Rumi describes the ascent of men to God through the various stages in these words:-

"From the inorganic we developed kingdom into the vegetable,
Dying from the vegetable we rose to animal,
And leaving the animal we became men,
Then what fear that death will lower us ?
The next transition will make us an angel,
Then shall we rise from angels and merge in the Nameless,

All existence proclaims, "Unto Him shall we return."

Union with God is the end of life. The Sufi Al-Hujviri says, "when a man becomes annihilated from his attributes he attains to perfect subsistence, he is neither near nor far, neither stranger nor intimate, neither sober nor intoxicated, neither separated nor united; he has no name or sign or brand or mark."(16) While the Sufi doctrine holds absorption in God as the goal of perfection, the Qu'ran gives us vivid pictures of the kind of life which the liberated enjoy. The descriptions of this life are realistic and somewhat sensuous too. They are not however to be literally interpreted. "O, thou soul which are at rest return unto thy Lord, pleased and pleasing Him, enter thou among my servants and enter thou my garden of felicity." (LXXXIX 27-30). The two views correspond to those held by the absolutistic and theistic interpretations of the Vedanta. The process of the growth of personality cannot stop until the end of perfection is reached and the future will have opportunities for the development of character.

The future depends on our present life. "Yonder will every soul experience that which it hath bargained for" (X 30). Paradise or hell is the result of our own actions. It is also sometimes urged that the silent inscrutable will of God directs all things. In the later history of Islam, the problem of the reconciliation of Divine sovereignty with human responsibility figures much. There are passages in the Qu'ran which seem to indicate that God acts in an arbitrary manner. "He pardons what He will and punishes whom he will in as much as God is a supreme sovereign." (II 184; See also III 25; V 18; XIII 31) "Verily God leads astray whomsoever He will and directs to Himself those who are penitent" (XIII 27). There are also passages which emphasise human responsibility. "No soul shall labour but for itself, and no burdened one shall bear another's burden." (II 286) "Whosoever gets to himself a sin, gets it solely on his own responsibility" (IX III). "Whoever goes astray, he himself bears the whole responsibility of wandering" (X 108). Sir Ahmed Hussain contends that fatalism is not a part of the Moslem creed (p 12 noted). "The Prophet distinctly taught that we should first of all do whatever lies in our power and then leave the rest to God. We are apt to forget the first part of his precept and cling to its second part only which accords with our tropical laziness." (p 62, note-b). Man is not the sport of fate. he has the freedom to choose the right or the wrong. God does not compel us to good or evil but shows us the way to truth and purity and helps us to observe the laws though He punishes us when we neglect them. Caliph Ali says : "O, Ye servants of my Lord, fulfil the duties that are imposed on you, for in their neglect is absement; your good works alone will render easy the road to death. Remember each sin increases the debt and makes the chain heavier. The message of mercy has come; the path of truth is clear; obey the command that has been laid on you; live in purity, work in piety and ask God to help you in every endeavour and to forgive your past transgressions."(17) The decrees of God are only the laws of the spiritual world. God helps those who seek His help and bestows grace on the penitent sinner who likes to purify his soul from impure longings. Caliph Ali says : "Say not that man is compelled, for that is attribution of tyranny to God, nor say that man has absolute discretion - rather that we are furthered by His help and grace in our endeavours to act righteously, and we transgress because of our neglect (of his commands)." (18)

Islam is a religion without mystery. Its simplicity is its strength and beauty. It does not indulge in any theological subtleties, supernatural paradoxes or metaphysical pretensions. It is natural religion with one central principle that God makes, upholds, govern and perfects all things. This serene lofty theism is best suited for the simple-minded and the unsophisticated. On its institutional side, it is perfectly rational. It has no caste or priests, requires no sacrifice or ceremonial, recognises no ritual likely to distract the mind, from the thought of the one God. Pilgrimage to Mecca and the shrine of Kaaba is the only external aid insisted on by Mohammad from a purely practical motive. During prayers, the Moslem turns his face towards Mecca, the glorious centre from which was announced first the gospel of Mohammad (Sura II 139, 144). Attention to Mecca helps the Moslem to realise that he is one of the band of the faithful, united by common allegiance to Mohammad as the Prophet of God, filled with the same hopes, reverencing the same thing, and worshipping the same ideals. Democracy is the keynote of Islam on its practical side. This is what enabled it to suceed as a missionary religion. It invites every human being to its ample fold, whatever be his colour or race. It recognises the capacity of all to become the servants of God.

"In each human spirit is a Christ concealed,
To be helped or hindered, to be hurt or healed.
If from any human soul you lift the veil,
*you will find a Christ there hidden without fail"**

The Moslems face without fear the logical implications of the doctrine of *Tat tvam asi* and make no distinctions between man and man, at any rate in their mosques. The same cannot be said of Hindu temples or Christian churches, in spite of all the lip homage paid to the principle of equality of all men in the eyes of God. The simple creed of Islam, careful of its two principles of Divine Fatherhood and human brotherhood has been potent enough to expel from many dark places of the earth, barbarous practices, and train millions of mankind to a better life. It has helped the backward races to escape from the labyrinth of sensuous polytheism and get rid of their devil worship and fetishism, infanticide and human sacrifices, magic and witchcraft. It will have a great future, if it cuts off with an unsparing hand the poisonous outgrowths and realises its two central principles in life.

Hinduism has not sufficiently profited from her experience of Islam. It is quite true the Reform movements such as those of Chaitanya, Kabir and Nanak were much influenced by the spirit of Islam. The monothesistic elements of Hinduism have become more emphasised after the spread of Islam in India. Yet Hinduism could easily have learnt more. Ignorance of others' faith is the mother of injustice and error. Some of the practices of the uncultured Moslems blinded the eyes of the Hindus to the ideals of Islam. While there is much for Islam to learn from a sympathetic understanding of Hinduism, there is also much for Hinduism to learn from Islam. For one thing, Hinduism must learn to be less compromising and more emphatic in its denunciation of imperfect conceptions of God and cruder modes of worship. Hinduism fondly believed that truth would slowly work its way and lower conceptions would be themselves repudiated. As surely as darkness flies before the rays of the Sun, Hinduism thought, so surely will falsehood vanish before truth. This has remained a pious hope. Those who are aware of the highest conceptions of God are found engrossed in the most revolting practices of barbarism. Those who glibly talk of **ahimsa** are seen encouraging animal sacrifices. Hinduism need not give up its tolerance but it should see to it that its judgement of values is kept up and progress is steadily achieved. We must also learn to democratise our institutions and do away with the wrangling creeds, unintelligible dogmas and oppressive institutions under which the soul of man is literally crushed. Both Islam and Hinduism at their best teach that true religion is to serve God in truth and purity and obey His laws reverently in all the affairs of life.

1. Note on Islam by Sir Ahmed Hussain, K. C. I. E., C. S. L., edited by Khan Bahadur Hajee Khaja Muhammad Hussain. Government Central press, Hyderabad, Deccan.
2. The Interpreters.
3. Masnair III 12.
4. The following pasago from Jalal-ud-din Rumi's Masnavi brings out how we should sympathise with cruder forms of worship, giving credit to thier sincerity.

   Moses, to his horror, heard one summer day
   A benightedshephered blashohemously pray
   'Lord', he said, 'I would I knew Thee, where Thou art,
   That for Thee I might perform a servant's part
   Comb thy hair, and dust Thy shoes and sweep Thy room
   Bring Thee every morning milk and honeycomb.'
   Moses cried,'Blasphemer ! curb thy blatant speech !
   Whom art thou addressing ? Lord of all and each,
   Allah the Almighty ? Thinkest thou He doth need
   Thine officous folly ? Wilt all bounds exceed ?
   Miscreat, have a care, lest thunderbolts should break
   On our heads and others perish for thy sake
   Without eyes He seeth, without ears He hears,
   Hath No son nor partner thorugh the endless years,
   pace cannot contain him time he is above
   All the limits that He knows are Light and Love !
   Put to shame, The Shepherd, his poor garment rent,
   Went away disheartened, all his ardour spent
   Then spake God to Moses : "Why hast thou from me
   Driven away my servant, who goes heavily ?
   Not for severince it was but union
   I Commissioned thee to preach, O hasty one !

hatefullest of all things is to me divorce,
And the worst of all ways is the way of force.
I made not creation, self to aggrandize
But that creatures might with me communion prize
What though the childish tongues trip ? 'Tis the heart I see, If it really loves me in sincerity.
Quoted in Blande Field's Mystics and Saints of Islam (p. 154.)

5. See also XXI 46, XXXII, 23, 24; XXXIX, 41; XL, 13,
6. Psalms.
7. Acts X, 34-35.
8. Amir Ali : The Spirit of Islam p. 212.
9. Calcutta Reviev, May 1923.
10. Asia, December 1922.
11. Kartum Akartum anyathakartum samarthah.
12. Quoted in The Spirit of Islam p. 416.
13. The Spirit of Islam. pp. 150, 157.
14. The Spirit of Islam, p. 54.
15. Ibid p. 158.
16. The Spirit of Islam p. 172. 213.
17. The Spirit of Islam p. 409
18. Ibil p. 410
19. Claude Field. the Mystics and Saints of Islam. p. 159.

HINDU THOUGHT & CHRISTIAN DOCTRINE

In a paper by Mr. Greaves on Hinduism contributed to the Oxford Conference,(1) it is said, 'Speakig broadly, Hindus are often about as far as in advance of the Hinduism they profess as are nominal Christians behind the Christianity which they are supposed to obey.' This judgement is a generous one, so far as Hindu practice is concerned, though its implication that Hindu thought is unworthy of this practice is open to question. We are all too ready to condemn what we do not understand and those who judge Hinduism from without are not able to understand its vitality. The great things for which men have lived and died, and are still living and dying, canot be grasped without the exercise of the spirit of what is well called 'natural piety.' If with this feeling we put ourselves at the point of view of the other religions, we shall see that the same fundamentals are found emphasised in all religions, that God is, that man stands in some relation to God, and that intercourse of some kind is possible between God and man who has in him the desire to be in harmony with God. The differences among the living progressive religions of the world relate to accents and emphases, which are traceable to social environments and historic circumstances. it is a matter of great satisfaction, that, under the impulse of higher criticism, the increasing knowledge of nature, idealist philosophy, comparative religion, the psychology of the religious consciousness and a deeper acquiantance with mystic experience, Christian thinkers are engaed in a re-construction of belief, that brings Christianity near the Hindu religion and promises to bridge the gulf that separates the Christian and the other religions. It is my endeavour in this paper to state briefly - a systematic discussion is not possible in a single article - some of the fundamentals of the Hindu faith so as to indicate its affinities to the Christian doctrine. By the fundamentals of Hinduism, I mean those common ideas which have characterised the different forms of Hinduism in their long history, regarding the problems of God, man and his future.

I

According to the Hindu view, the mystery of God cannot be comprehended by the mind of man. Many scriptural texts lay stress on the inadequacy of the finite mind to the subtlety of God's nature. There are endless attributes and aspects in the Supreme of which we, human beings, have no knowledge. No Hindu, however, rests content with this negative view. he insists on interpreting the nature of God on the analogy of his own personality, which is a complex of cognitions, affections and desires. He speaks of God as a personal being, *purusha*, with qualities of thought, love and power. All the time, he is conscious that God's personality is only a mask, the revelation of something higher under this form. God's personality is not the limited and exclusive one which the human is, for in God we live, move, and have our being.

Since God's personality is the unity of wisdom, love and goodness, His activities in relation to the world are those of creation, redemption and judgement. *Brahma*, representing the cognitive aspect of God, creates; Vishnu, representing God as love, redeems; Siva, who is God as omnipotent power and perfection, judges. The order of the universe reflects the mind of God. The transformation of the eternal ideas of God into the plane of space-time is a gradual one. All things struggle continuously to get rid of their imperfections that they might conform to their eternal archetypes, that is, realise God's purpose for them. The cosmic pRocess is a continuous evolution where things develop new and higher qualities in conflict with the old ones. The conception of *Brahma* brings out the infinitude of God and His unceasing creative activity. The aim of God's creation is the manifestation by His creatures of their divine origin and destiny. Of all objects of God's creation only man can manifest fully the character of his origin and reveal the truth of things. God, when He created man, presented to him the ideal which he should elect, the law which he should obey, if he is to realise his destiny. The Bhagavadgita (III 10) says, '*Brahma* created man along with the law of sacrifice.' The law is the means by which we can realise God's ideal for us and grow into His likeness. but we forget our origin, forget our place in the plan of God, forget the law of sacrifice, and lose ourselves in selfish pursuits. It is then that the need for God's redemptive power arises. The All-great *Brahma* is the All-loving Vishnu too. His love and grace are around us, behind what appears as space-time, the material world, organic life and human history. *Vishnu* the All-pervading, actively helps every human soul to fight against sin and stupidity. He is the central core of our being, serving as an inner light, which is too holy to consent to any evil, too real to cling to the fleeting and too loving to regard anything as alien to itself. He is God the redeemer and is the security that the World is progressing towards the good. But He does not act against our will. His redemptive activity takes place in accordance with the order created by *Brahma.* God does not care to exalt Himself by condemning the laws of creation which his own fingers framed. Though *Vishnu* is ever ready to help us, our sin and stupidity constitute barriers against the operation of His grace. Even though we have sinned and thus betrayed the God in us, yet if we turn to God in faith, he helps us out of our difficulty. 'Even if the very wicked worship me, with devotion to none else, he should be regarded as good, for he has rightly resolved. Soon does he become righteous and attain to eternal peace. Boldly canst thou proclaim that my devotee is never destroyed,' says Krishna in the Gita.(2) There is thus a chance for even the worst sinner. God is not merely truth and love, but also justice. He is the embodiment of power and perfection, the judge of good and evil, the lord of karma, **karmadhyaksah**. When we sin, it is Siva the judge, who punishes us.

Brahma, Vishnu and **Siva** are not three different persons but three aspects of one God, who has no second, distinguished according to His different functions. **Brahma** creates us with certain potentialities, **Vishnu** helps us to realise them through the overcoming of opposition and **Siva** signifies the victorious self-maintenance of the good. As the **Tatttiriya Upanishad** puts it, 'the source from which things come, that by which they are sustained and into which they enter' are one. God is the truth, the way and the life. He is one viewed as threefold, **eka eva tridha smratah**. Creation, redemption and judgement are the three fundamental aspects of the creative evolution.

When we regard the Supreme as Divine self conciousness functioning in the three ways of creation, redemption and judgement, it follows that the world with reference to which these functions have a meaning, is organically related with God. The world is the body of the God, according to some **Upanishads**, the **Bhagvadagita** and theistic **Vedanta**. Hindu thought is not afraid of asserting the presence of

God in all things. It has no faith in a transcendent God distinct from the world, living in a monotonous solitude of His own. Krishna says in the Gita, that all the beauty of the world, all its truth, all its goodness are so many modes in which God is manifested, of whose glory nature is the veil, of whose word it is the expression, of whose thought it is the embodiment. This, however, is not pantheism in the crude sense of the term. Distinctions are made between the ideal and the actual, the good and its opposite. Hinduism insists on the need for self-transcendence on the part of man. This means that there is something beyond what actually is, that man is struggling to realise. The necessity for redemption shows that there are elements from which we are to be redeemed. If all that is, is equally divine, there would be no need for redemption or judgement. God is not only in nature as its life but is beyond it, as its Creator, its Lord and its Judge. Hinduism does not subscribe to the Hegelian identification of the process of the world with the life of the Absolute. The world is rooted in God, but God does not die if the world perishes. In His own being He is independent of the world and abvoe it. His spirit moves in the world, informing it, governing it, and yet it is by itself beyond it all.

That the water of a stream is purer at its source is certainly true of the religion of Christianity. If we turn to the life and sayings of Jesus, we get a clear idea of the central principles of Christianity. Yahweh of the Old Testament was essentially a national deity. Though some prophets like Hosea and Isaiah regarded Him as the God of the whole earth, they did not altogether escape from their provincial views. Even for them Israel remained God's chosen race and the heathen nations who would submit to His authority and come to worship at Zion would occupy a position of subjection. Jesus purged the idea of God of all particularism. He was not much interest in God as He is in Himself but revealed to us with remarkable insight the nature of God in relation to man and the world. Though Jesus referred to the three aspects of wisdom, love and power, the then conditions led him to emphasise the love of God. Even the better class of Jewish prophets exaggerated the aspect of God's judgement and His wrath. Isaiah says: 'Men shall go into the caves of the rocks, and into the holes of the earth from before the terror of the Lord, and from the glory of His majesty, when he ariseth to shake mightily the earth' and Jesus laid stress on the conception of God as Father and his love for us as His children, God is pre-eminently love. He is our redeemer, but the other aspects were not neglected by Jesus. The orderliness of the world reveals the wisdom of God. The Sun shines impartially on the just and the unjust, and so does the rain fall. Special providences are not accepted by Jesus(3) who rebukes the petty egotism which imagines that the natural order of the universe is interrupted to inflict exemplary punishments on evil doers or bring rich rewards to individuals of exeptional merit. He refused to succumb to the temptation to make stones into bread. The physical cures which He effected were all according to law and he could not heal where faith was lacking. God is unalterable truth, and His universe cannot be an anarchic one. God is also the judge. The judgement of God is the dominating note of the Bible. From the sentence upon Adam and Eve and the condemnation of Cain, down to the closing vision of St. John's Apocalypse, we have stress on the sovereignty and judgement of God. At the end of the day, it is God's purpose that will triumph. The Christian Church, in the spirit of the Hebrew prophets appeals more to the terror of judgement and the wrath of God than to the sense of guilt and the grace of God.

When the followers of Jesus raised Jesus to the rank of God, the three aspects of **Brahma, Viṣhnu** and **Siva,** infinitude, grace and sovereignty, wisdom, love and power were attributed to Him. He is Logos or Wisdom or Word of God, who was before Abraham was. He is the Saviour who revealed His heart of love on the cross at Calvary. He is the judge who pronounces sentence on all who offend Him. 'He that cometh after me, says John the Baptist, 'will gather up his wheat into the garner but the chaff He will burn up with unquenchable fire.' He will separate the sheep from the goats.'(4)

The doctrine of the Trinity not only sought to provide a place for Jesus in the unity of God but also tried to correct the onesided view of God adopted in the Old Testament. God is not merely the infinite majesty seated on high (the Father), but is also the heart of love (the Son), and the immanent principle of the world process (the Holy Spirit). God is not the transcendent, remote from the world, but Infinite love who pours Himself out unweariyingly into the uplift of the world. Abelard and, in a manner, Aquinas support the view of the Father as power, the old Yahweh exercising judgement *(siva)*, the Son as the Logos, Word or Wisdom, the principle of creation *(Brahma)*, and the Holy Spirit as pervading love *(Vishnu)*. On this view, the Father, the Son and the Holy Spirit correspond to the Vedantic formula of Brahman as **Sat, Chit**, and **Ananda** reality, wisdom and joy. One thing is clear, that the doctrine of the Trinity is an attempt to indicate the threefold nature of God. Modern Christian theology is realising that the unity of God is consistent with his three aspects, only if the latter are regarded as modes of His activity and not as three different minds or centres of consciousness.

It is frequently urged that the Hindu view exaggerates the justice of God while the Christian lays more stress on the love of God. This is however not altogether just. There is not much real difference on this question, between the two views. Vishnu, or God as love, is ready to help us but He waits for our effort. He does not offer His aid against our will. He cannot save us even when we sin, unless we repent. God will do everything for us, but if we persist in our sin and selfishness and do not turn to Him, law will have its course. God cannot deny Himself. he would like to forgive all but there are sins which 'shall not be forgiven, neither in this world nor in that which is to come.' Even the love of God has a method according to which it works. We cannot say that this constitutes a limitation of His power. Omnipotence is not irrationality. Jesus recognises that there are laws of the spiritual world. The parables of the tares, the thief, the hidden treasure, the pearl, the lost(5) sheep, the talents, the ten virgins and the wedding garment, all imply the law that we shall be saved only by our deeds. The five foolish virgins failed to use their opportunities and so missed their end. If we expect forgiveness, we must forgive; if we would save our lives, we must lose them. Such as the inexorable laws of the spiritual world which even God's love cannot set aside. Salvation is to be earned; God cannot thrust it on us. The implication of the curious doctrine of vicarious sacrifice is that the love of God is tempered by His justice. It assumes that divine justice must be satisfied before God can forgive.

Western Christianity is a product of several influences. Its Jewish heritage which conflicts with the Greek, inclines it to support the transcendent conception of God. For the Jew as well as the Arab, nature seemed dry and barren;

to the Greek as to the Hindu it was alive and divine. The latter did not exaggerate the distinction between the sacred and the profane, the nature and the supernatural, the spirit and the flesh, Their general conception is confirmed by the spirit of science with its insistence on the essential unity of nature. The all-pervading supremacy of law keeps the lawless at arm's length. The supernatural is at the heart of nature. As Aristotle said, spirit is the form of matter. God is the life of the world. The growing appreciation of the meaning of history and the principle of development, the fresh psychological analysis of the religious consciousness and its growths incline us to see the divine in the normal and not in deviations from it. The view of God, as one who acts upon the world externally, moulding it as a potter does clay, which has had a continuous history in Christendom from Jesus - even He was fettered much by His religious surroundings - through Paul, Augustine, Luther, Calvin etc. is slowly yielding to a more immanent conception. A whole-hearted acceptance of Divine immanence will involve much doctrinal re-adjustment and many of the sacred sentiments which have twined themselves round the old idea will have to be given up. We cannot accept Divine immanence and yet be conventionally orthodox, clinging to the reality of miracles, chosen people, exclusive mediatorship, unique revelations, salvation by grace rather than by development, and damnation at death for the large majority of the human race. Christian theologians are accepting the view of immanence with different degrees of completeness. Though Jesus was much hampered by his Jewish heritage, He yet had a fine faith in God as the indwelling presence in the world. The kingdom of God is within you.' With the Hindu, Jesus believes that the changes of the world are not the results of an occasional interference of God from outside, but are a regular divine progress. The central lesson of the life of Jesus to the Hindu is the undermining of the false antithesis between man and God. Jesus is the example of a man who has become God and none can say where his manhood ends and divinity begins. Man and God are akin. 'That art Thou.' *Tat tvam asi.*

II

The doctrine of the immanence of God in life and history is inconsistent with the theory of unique revelations at particular epochs. Hinduism prefers to think of God's activity as immanent in the whole spiritual development of the race. It yet tickets off some prominent aspects of this continuous development, as indicating in a more striking manner the presence of God. Though divine life permeates, subdues and controls all life on earth, still, the stages, when the higher forms were evolved, when the better types were perfected, reveal more prominently the working of the immanent spirit. The stages are marked by the appearance of the subhuman *avatars*. When man appears on the scene, the problem of morality arises and the continuous redemptive activity of God becomes more manifest when the moral order is sharply disturbed. The restoration of the moral equilibrium demands the appearance of some who embody greater goodness than usual.(6) These souls who support unflinchingly the cause of God, that is goodness reveal more than ordinary beings, the eternal within the temporal, the grain within the husk. These manifestations of spiritual values may be viewed either as the revelation of God or the realisation of the potentiialities of man, since these two are different ways of stating one fact. We call them fresh revelations of the depths of God or decisive developments of possibilities of man. Naturally, the pious view them as deliberate acts of God adopted in divine wisdom to serve His purpose. But the higher thought of India is emphatically of opinion, that God is ever active and love is His very essence and not a mere accidental aberration.

While all men reproduce or incarnate to some extent the nature of God, His truth, love and power, those who are called *avatars* do so in a more stiking way and to a greater degree. This is the case with Rama, Krishna and Buddha. Jesus is an *avatar* since His love for the sinful which came out most markedly in his appeal on the Cross, 'Father forgive them for they know not what they do' is of a piece with God's love for His children. But that He had a special relation to God, which it is not possible for others to acquire is a proposition which it is very difficult to defend. nor is there any authentic evidence of it, I venture to submit, in the synoptic Gospels. Stories, of course, there are, as about many others in the pre-Christian and the post-Christian eras, but on such a question they count for little. The Adoptionist Christology and the Pre-existence theory involve an untenable antithesis between God and man, which is reminiscent of Jewish dualism. The life of Jesus will have no meaning for us, if He had any non-human elements which enabled Him to reach perfection. Faith in the Fatherhood of God compels us to assume that what was possible for Jesus is also possible for other men. The resources of God which were available to Him are open to us, and if we struggle and strive even as He did, we will develop the God in us. We are all partakers of God's nature and can incarnate God's love even as Jesus did, if we acquire Jesus' faith in God. At best, Jesus is 'the first born among many brethren.'(7) The incarnation of God in Jesus is essentially one with the indwelling of

God in the other saints of the world. The divine relationship revealed by Him is potentially present in all of us. It is a pious delusion to think that none else than Jesus attained this consciousness of spiritual oneness with God. The history of Hinduism gives several instances of souls who were saved, who had the experience of the oneness of 'I and my Father,' who saw with the eye of the soul the glory of God as it is in its own nature, not merely as momentary gleams breaking though the darkness of the sense world, and enjoyed Him for ever. The nearer the approach to God, the greater is the community of nature between man and God and he who lives in God, not intermittently but constantly can say, 'I am He.'

The testimony of the *Rishis* of the *Upanishads* is confirmed by Jesus and other religious geniuses of the world. Let us hear the Sufi martyr, Al Hallaj : 'I am the Truth; I am He whom I love; and He whom I love is I. We are two souls dwelling in one body. when thou seest me, thou seest Him, and when thou seest Him, thou seest me.' In that condition of at-one-ment, there is no opposition between the human soul and divine. According to Jami : "'I' and 'Thou' have here no place, and are but phantasies vain and unreal."(8)

In our loyalty and devotion to Jesus, we may say that the revelation of God in Jesus is a perfect and complete one and His personality is unapproached in all history. The light of God, it is admitted sometimes with great reluctance, shone clearly no doubt, in some prophetic souls, but it never blazed forth in such unique splendour as in Jesus. All this may be true, but we cannot legitimately object, if the followers, say of Confucius and of Buddha, set up similar claims for their heroes. If it is argued that spiritual experience on a vast scale confirms the divinity and mediatorship of Jesus, similar experience is not wanting for the other great saviours of humanity. Hinduism believes that every *guru* is a saviour inasmuch as he quickens in his disciples the life of God, and develops the seed of the spirit, capable of fructifying in them. Any one who helps us to a complete harmonisation of the finite will of man with the perfect will of God has the power to save us. In some systems like that of the *Saiva Siddhanta*, the *guru* is said to be the very God who appears out of the fulness of His grace to help man in the upward *ascent*. It cannot be contended that it is impossible to reach heaven unless it be through the mediatorship of Jesus. It is even admitted that Abraham got there, centuries before Jesus was born.(9)

It is not easy to follow such a proposition as that all ideal qualities of perfect manhood for all time and all conditions were included in Jesus and His revelation is final and all inclusive. There is no finality with regard to any revelation on earth. God has never said His last word on any subject. he has always more things to tell us than we now can bear.(10)

A more critical attitude towards the divinity of Jesus is growing among the Christian theologians of the West, who are tending to emphasize more and more the humanity of Jesus. The claims to omniscience and the consciousness of having created the universe are not seriously pressed. On the other hand, more attention is paid to the statements that He 'grew in wisdom,' 'learned obedience by the things which he suffered,' was made 'perfect through sufferings,' and 'hath been in all points tempted as we are.' The travail of the spirit in the wilderness makes Him our brother. he like us, felt in the presence of the great God that lovely reverence and humility which made Him say, 'Why callest thou me good. There is none good but One, that is, God.' 'My father is greater than I.'(11) Miracles are not adduced as evidence of His divinity. Science is critical of many of them. Psychotherapy is able to explain a few. Jesus Himself never designed to perform miracles to prove His divinity. On the other hand, He admits that others also are able to do them. 'If I by Beelzebub cast out devils, by whom do your sons cast them out ?'(12) Jesus' own testimony, philosophical truth, and religious experience alike demand that Jesus should be brought into line with the other great saints of God, who has not left Himself without a witness in any clime or age.

III

Man is made in the image of God and so is not naturally deprived. As we now find him, he is, no doubt, handicapped in several ways. These defects are foreign to his true nature and are the result of his abuse of freedom. The Hebrew story

'Of man's first disobedience, and the fruit
Of that forbidden tree whose mortal taste
Brought death into the world and all our woe'

endorses the Hindu view that sorrow and suffering, consequent on sin and stupidity, are produced by man, though God allowed them when he gave us freedom. God, as we saw, does not deal with us as a potter with clay but gave us full freedom to realise our destiny, but man loved his false self and not his true self and source, God, and thus evil arose. Our sinfulness however does not destroy the immortal glory that is our heritage though it postpones its arrival.

The doctrine of the natural depravity of man, I fear, cannot be sustained. The divine is our nature. The light of God lighteth every man who cometh into the world. 'Thou wouldst not be seeking me if thou didst not possess me.' Goethe says :

'Were not the eye itself a Sun
No Sun for it could ever shine,
By nothing Godlike could the heart be won
Were not the heart itself divine.'

On this view, conversion is not the birth of anything new, though it is the sudden reversal of the former course of life. Salvation is more a gradual development of the divine in us than a gift due to the grace of God. Modern psychological analysis of the act of redemption informs us that God acts in the development of the individual soul more from within than from without. Grace and development are two aspects of one process though the former suggests something like a spiritual miracle or crisis and the latter implies the continuity of man and God.

The course of discipline which the individual is called upon to undergo, if he is to realise his divine inheritance may be distinguished into three types, answering to the three aspects of conscious life. In the period of the *Upanishads*, God was regarded primarily as Eternal Truth or Light and the individual was asked to comprehend the nature of God by *sraddha* or faith and *jnana* or wisdom. When we pass to the Bhagavadgita, it is the aspect of God as love that becomes more prominent and *bhakti* or devotion to God becomes the chief means of salvation. With the Buddists and the Saivites, as with the ancient Hebrews, God is the Eternal Righteousness and *tapas* or austere simplicity of life and self-sacrifice become emphasised. Any one of these three methods *jnana, bhakti* or *tapas* has the power to transform our life as a whole.

When we undergo this inward renewal of mind, heart and will, when we give up our self-regarding life, we find one which beats in unison with the impersonal and the universal good. This is to be saved. The secret of salvation is not a change of creed but an inward renewal. The kingdom of God is an attitude of the soul. Salvation is a qualitative change which fills the life of man with the spirit of God. What the exact nature of it is, cannot be translated into our terms, coined as they are in the mint of human experence. The glory that shall be, we cannot know fully. If we insist on interpreting the nature of eternal life in he language of logic and time, we have to say that it is an identification of the will of the soul with that of God, or more concretely, it is citizenship in the kingdom of God or *Brahmaloka,* from which there is, no possibility of degradation into the world of samsara. *Sankara* declares the impossibility of characterising the supreme experience of oneness with God and allows, if any logical description is demanded, that it is best to say that that life is dwelling in the city of God. Ramanuja, however, believes that nothing higher is conceivable or real.

The ascended Christ says : 'I will make him a pillar in the temple of my God and he shall go no more out.'(13) The expression that '*he shall go no more out*' has a family likeness to the Hindu view that the saved soul does not return to the struggle of *samsara. Napunnravrittih.* Both the Hindu and the Christian views agree with regard to the features of the free souls. Wisdom, love and joy are the fruits of salvation. The saved soul has that perfect confidence in the goodness of things that he is not tossed about by the winds of doctrine and dogma. He has that true love or inward brotherliness. It is not mere refraining from injury or forgiveness of enemies, but positive service of humanity. No great religious leader has failed to pay his homage to the principle of love. *Ahimsa* is a central feature of the ethics of the *Upanishads*. Buddha asks us to do good to them that hate us. In the Book of Exodus, we read, 'If thou meet thine enemy's ox or his ass going astray, thou shalt surely bring it back to him.' The forty-fifth chapter of Genesis gives us an idea of the admiration which the ancients had for a magnanimous man. See the superb scene in which Joseph forgives his brethren. Paul quotes from the Book of Proverbs, when he writes to the Romans' If thine enemy hunger, feed him; if he thirst, give him to drink.' Of Jesus, it is said, 'Who, when he was reviled, reviled not again, when he suffered, threatened not.'(14) The saved soul has not only wisdom and love but also that real joy which is not at the mercy of men and circumstances, the peace or *santi* of which the Hindus speak. It is the joy to which Jesus referred when he said: 'My joy I give unto you, and your joy no man taketh from you.'

Apparently there is not very much serious difference between Hinduism and Christianity on the question of the nature and means of salvation, if we do not take into account the doctrine of Atonement, that 'God was in Christ reconciling the world unto Himself.' That Jesus helps us to turn away from sin and towards God, as every saint, in some degree, does, is beyond question. But the sacrifice of Christ has no significace for man as a propitiation for sin. Jesus is our Saviour since He gives us evidence in his life of the love of God, which will bear us in all crises and catastrophes.

He gives us assurance that it is possible for us to conquer the world, the flesh and the devil and attain perfection. Ritschl rightly contends, "All that we can recognise as the real truth of His existence, is that through the impulse and direction we receive from Him, it is possible for us to enter into His relation to God and the world. (15)

IV

The doctrines of *karma* and re-birth which distinguish the faith of the Hindus, do not evidently commend themselves to the majority of Christian thinkers who, I am afraid, are mostly misled by misrepresentations. *Moksha* or at-one-moment with God is not possible as long as the individual clings to his separate narrow individuality. Until all traces of this separatist tendency are suppressed, union with the Supreme cannot be realised. We are committed to the world of *samsara* the endless cycle of lives, until we conquer time and reach perfection. This view is not so fantastic as it is generally said to be. If life eternal (*moksha*) means a state which transcends temporal conditions (*samsara*), then so long as we cling to the latter, time, the former, eternity, cannot be attained. Unless we drop the individual point of view and raise ourselves to the universal, we cannot lay hold on the truth. All our efforts to reach the universal standpoint, while retaining the individual, are doomed to disappointment. Moral growth is of this character. It has for its basis the exclusive individual with separate plans, purposes and preferences, confronted by others with similar interests. Through moral effort, the individual can approximate to the goal but never reach it. *Samsara* is the world of individualistic moralism which, has for its principle perpetual progress or endless growth and not effective realisation of complete fruition. Kant's ethics gives us an instructive analogy. The imperative of the moral law demands a total suppression of the sensitive part of man's nature. This end is not realised in our present experience, and so he offers us an infinite future to realise it, but Kant forgets that infinite time is inadequate for an impossible task. *Finite* agents cannot achieve *infinite* perfection, even if they groan and travail to the end of time. Kant prescribes a self-contradictory task. The way out is to knock down the sense of the finite. Only then can we be saved from the unending progress of the finite which yields no satisfaction. Unless we abandon the standpoint of *samsara* by cutting through the chain and lift ourselves up above sensitivity, above space-time, above individuality, there is no release possible. Life eternal can be lived here, and now, if only we discard the separatist viewpoint of mere moralism and rise to the religious level.

In the world of *samsara*, the law of *karma* holds. It is the principle of moral continuity by which all steps on the upward path which we gain through toil and suffering are secured for us, and the character we build conserved, so that we need not re-travace old steps but always look upwards and onwards. According to the doctrine of *karma*, every man will have chances opened to him until he realises the destiny for which he is intended. If God is love, none can be lost for ever. The redemptive work of God does not cease, until the purpose of God is fulfilled with regard to every thing. The sin of man hides but does not destroy his immortal destiny. God's love would not allow even the worst sinner to slip away from Him completely. If death were the end, God's purpose in creating us would be frustrated; for most of us die unrepentant and in sin. If we do not admit the defeat of God's purpose, which would be a very serious limitation of God's nature, then there must be scope for growth, after death, for all souls, to develop and manifest the God in them. This view seems to be much more consistent with the justice and love of God than the one prevailing in Christendom, which has adopted a hell for the large majority of mankind. A deeper realization of the truth of God as love will lead Christian thinkers to admit development after death.

If God destroys his delinquent children, then we are attributing to God a very primitive instinct which even civilised men have sublimated. If Jesus took little children on His knees and told His hearers that the only way of pleasing God was to become themselves like little children, it is atrocious for us to thrust these citizens of the kingdom of heaven into the fire of hell.

According to St. Paul, 'the whole creation groaneth and travaileth in pain together... waiting for the manifestation of the sons of God.' If any souls are doomed for ever without a chance of manifesting themselves as sons of God, then God's ideal consummation for the world has broken down. The doctrine of divine immanence requires us to believe that no man deserves to be thrown into eternal hell. however far he may go astray, he is not a lost soul. None can shake off the divinity in him, however much he may hide it by his sin, stupidity and selfishness. The unsupported finite, the individual who is not rooted in the eternal, in other words, the man who is not made by God is the only rubbish fit to be cast into hell-fire, but not he who bears the human face divine. He may sin grossly in the life but his immortal destiny cannot be destroyed. Beneath the horrible mask of a Judas, there is the potentially divine face of a Jesus. St. Paul says : 'A veil lieth upon their heart. But whensoever a man shall turn unto the Lord, the veil shall be taken away,' Mark the words **'whensoever a man shall turn unto the Lord,'** that is, at any time in the history of the individual, in this world or in the world to come, if he repents he has a chance. To the Hindu, the case of Dives seems to be the height of tragedy.(16) In a repentant mood, he begs for a small favour, and that not for himself, and no God cares to listen to his prayer. For there is no escape possible for a soul tormenting in hell. Once dead, the fate of man seems to be settled eternally. Assuming that God is not love, but stern justice with fierce indignation against wrong, the treatment of Dives is not even just. Errors unrepented of in this life cannot be punished through all the ages. But even the Old Testament gets over the conception of God as mere justice. Some of the Prophets and Psalmists had a more adequate view. 'The Lord is merciful and gracious, slow to anger and plenteous in mercy.(17) With such a God who is ready to forgive and welcome back the sinner, Dives has a chance. 'How much more' has he with Jesus' God who is not only the Father who waits at home to receive the prodigal, but also the Shepherd who searches in the mountains for the lost sheep ? If God goes out to seek the sinner and bring him back, the repentance of Dives will be a matter of rejoicing to Him. If God is unimaginably good' exceeding abundantly above all we can ask or think,' is this hope of a future, where souls like Dives could develop in their new mood, too good to be true ? 'If ye then, being evil, know how to give good gifts unto your children, how much more shall your Father which is in Heaven, give good things to those that ask Him !"(18) If we never can forgive as much as we have been forgiven, then is it right to think that God will not refrain from vengenance? God's illimitable love is the guarantee that there is a boundless future opening before us.

Except for the proposition that God is not the God of the dead but of the living, Jesus did not give any definite account of the future life. His references to it in the parables of the Sheep and the Goats, Dives and Lazarus are coloured by the beliefs of the age in heaven and hell, as geographical areas, full of blessedness and misery, and they are not relevant to the problem. Jesus evidently did not believe in a long interval between death and judgement for the rich glutton and Lazarus had their punishment and reward almost immediately after death. Jesus was not misleading the repentant theif when He said, 'To-day shalt thou be with me in paradise.'(19) The official view that the dead will rise with their physical bodies for judgement after death is not supported by these statements of Jesus.

On the orthodox view, it is difficult to know how it fares with the countless dead, in the interval between death and judgement. The only interpretation of heaven and hell consistent with the teaching and character of Jesus is that they refer to qualitative changes in the souls. Heaven symbolises the improvement of the soul and hell its opposite. And there are grades in hell, as well as in heaven, many mansions in God's Kingdom and each man will go to his place in accordance with the strength of his faith and the merit of his life. This is the way in which God's justice operates, as the law of *karma* tells us. As a man uses his chance, so will his progress be and the kind and extent of his use will determine his grade of development. That Jesus had a clear consciousness of the law of spiritual continuity comes out in many of his utterances. He is aware that men shall give account for every idle word which they speak on the day of judgement. All our nameless acts of tenderness and love - 'I was an hungered and ye gave me meat' - are quite effective in their results. As the **Bhagavadgita** says, 'even a little good saves us from great fear.' (II 40).

This view is in accord with the known facts of the development of human personality. The advance in holiness or perfection is a gradual moral process which cannot be achieved instantaneously. In normal circumstances self-development is a continuous process, with no conceivable limits. Growth is the law of personality and for it, both time and opportunity are necessay. The law of *karma* opens up a vast vista where there will be ample scope for self-development.

This principle rightly insists that our conduct as a whole determines our future. A single incident like baptism does not decide the fate of the individual. The infant which dies soon after baptism and the one without it, will both have practically the same future careers, other things remaining equal. Jesus would certainly be shocked to hear, that, according to his message of love, the penalty for error of belief, or accident of birth in another religion or the misfortune of missing some magical sacrament is continuous burning in hell-fire. It is spiritual growth that a man has made or failed to make that determines his future destiny.

The law of **karma** is criticised as being too mechanical and inconsistent with Divine love. The conception of God as an unfettered despot, who interferes whenever it pleases Him to make certain people sinful and others saintly, is repugnant to Hindu thought. To argue that God's love is not bound by the law of character is to support the Calvinistic theology of arbitrary and irrational decrees, according to which the elect shall be saved, do what they will, and the reprobate shall be damned, do what they can. It is impossible for God to ignore the conduct of men, though His love is so infiite that it supports all who make a start in the right direction. The necessities of the spiritual world demand that repentance should be followed by the forgiveness of sins and that utter self-surrender shall be followed by the grace of God. The moral law is the very being of God and it demands that the experiences to which we shall be subjected shall vary with the moral quality of our deeds. The constancy of God is not opposed to the love of God. The theory of divine immanence tells us that God's judgement does not come from anything external. It works from within. We raise or degrade ourselves by our acts. There is no escape from the law of God, which is closer to us than hands and feet, and is in fact the essence of us all. The law of *karma* tells us that those who violate God's laws must suffer for their violation, though there is possibility of repentance and improvement at every stage.

Those who argue that the Hindu doctrine of *karma* is mechanical because the absoluteness of the law demands that the full debt must be paid, uphold, rather strangely, a worse proposition that it must be paid, somehow, by somebody, if not by the sinner. That one man should suffer for another's sins is intelligible, whatever be its validity. But does not the situation become paradoxical, if not grotesque, when the sinner complacently accepts that another should suffer for his sin ? The view deludes the unthinking into the false notion that they might continue their careers of crime, for God would some day send some angel or Son of His to bear the sin of the world. The way in which orthodox Christian doctrine regards the suffering and death of Jesus, the guiltless victim, is conceivable only if God were a well-made weighing machine. I believe that it is intended to indicate the truth of the Hindu view that love of god and effort on the part of man are both necessary for moral growth.

It is well known that the theory of *karma* is set forth as an explanation for human inequality. Experience shows that all men are not equally favoured in inward disposition or outward circumstances. Heredity and environment contribute materially to the shaping of human souls. If we believe, as Calvin assuredly did, that the world is governed by a loving and intelligent being, we must admit that the diversities of life are not due to accident. Thus far the Hindu can follow the argument; but when Calvin suggests as a solution the theory of election, that the capricious will of God is responsible for the choice of some for salvation and others for perdition, the Hindu hesitates to follow his lead and asks whether there is not a more reasonable alternative. There is no need to adopt such a mechanical view of the relation of God to man. The law of *karma* traces this diversity of endowment to the ordered will of god. The Hindu is not prepared to introduce into the nature of God an element of utter irrationality. He believes that one increasing purpose manifests itself in the evolution of the universe, and if some become more readily the channels of divine grace than others, it is because they struggled a good deal to earn it in the past. 'Whatsoever a man soweth, that shall he also reap' says St. Paul. The law of *karma* accepts this principle and extends it further and says, 'Whatsoever a man reaps, that he must have sown.' Jesus, to my mind, understood this further implication. When he told the paralytic, 'Courage, my son, your sins are forgiven.' he meant to convey that his suffering was the result of his past sins.

The sinner may have forgotten them, but not God. The effects of his sins were lying in the depths of his personality. As modern psychology would say, our past deeds are stored up in the region of the unconscious. Jesus assumes something like the law of *karma*, when he tells the sick man 'sin no more, lest a worse thing come unto thee.' (St. John v. 14). Suffering is not the arbitray fiat of a judge who inflicts it on us, though we do not deserve it. Suffering forced on us against our will is the wages of sin. We cannot esteem it a privilege and an honour. In that case, those suffering in hell have no reason to be ashamed of themselves. Jesus recognised the value of suffering as a warning against evil and an incentive to good. All this does not apply to suffering voluntarily undertaken. Suffering is for purification until we realise life eternal. When we are perfected we become sharars in the work of God, which is the creation and maintenance of absolute values. Thereafter, all 'suffering' is self-imposed though it is quite distinct in its character from ordinary suffering. *Siva* drank poison for the redemption of mankind. Buddha, according to the Mahayana faith, refused to attain nirvana for the sake of man. In addition to (1) suffering inflicted on mortals as a punishment for their past sins and (2) 'suffering' seemingly so, undertaken by the free souls of the world, there is a third variety which is called *tapas* in hindu thought. Tapas is the suffering voluntarily undertaken by those who are still on the path way to perfection, for the sake of self-development or world welfare. This is a very difficult undertaking and some of the greatest souls of the world have quailed before it. Witness the scene at Gethsemane. To realise our destiny, the most efficient method is this suffering for the world. *Siva* the prince of ascetics, or God as Righteousness, expects of His devotees, austere asceticism and self-sacrifice, even as *Brahma* demands meditation and *Vishnu*, devotion. Suffering for the world out of love for it is the price which every son of man has to pay, if he is to be redeemed from evil and manifest himself as a son of God. The Cross is not an offence or a stumbling block to the Hindu, but is the great symbol of the redemptive reality of God. It shows how love is rooted in self-sacrifice. The story of Hinduism has many instances of Rishis and Buddhas who have sanctified *tapas* and suffered more than they deserved for the sake of the world. This avoidable suffering is not the result of past sins.

Christian thinkers have felt for long uneasy about the doctrine of perpetual torment and devised various schemes which would allow scope for future development. The Council of Florence in 1429 formulated the doctrine of purgatory which is neither hell nor heaven. Dean Farrar suggested an intermediate state of probation in which souls would have an opportunity for repentance. Some theologians take their stand on the vague statements of Peter iii, 19; iv 6, and argue for an intermediate state between death and judgement. While many plead for continuity between this life and the next, only very few are willing to advocate pre-existence. In course of time, however, Western thinkers will be led to discern the elements of value in the Hindu view, which is to-day confused with a good deal of grotesque mythology which no thinking Hindu accepts as literal truth.

V

Indian Christians who breathe the same spiritual air laden with the fragrance of India's past, as their Hindu brethren are deeply imbued with the doctrine of divine immanence.

It is becoming increasingly difficult for them to accept the apocalyptic view of the sternness of God and his supernaturalism which threatens disobedience of God's will with tremendously terriffic judgements, which looks upon Jesus as the very God of God sent to the world to be crucified as an atonement for the sins of mankind, and contemplates the renewal on a vast scale of the miracle of the resurrection, the coming of Christ in glory on a world which has rejected Him. The thoughtful, especially among the younger generation of Indian Christians, believe that God works in all men and in the whole world, though Jesus so perfected His nature that He manifested the God in him in a more marked degree than other men. They, of course, think that the life of Jesus which brought out the aspect of redeeming love in the nature of God which was practically ignored by the Old Testament writers, though some of their great prophets like Isaiah were not unaware of it, has the highest ethical significance for us in the present condition of the world. They confidently anticipate the coming of the kingdom of God by the gradual growth of goodness and spread of Christian love though not doctrine. They are deeply concerned when such vital doctrines of Hinduism as the unity and omnipenetrativeness of God, *ahimsa*, *karma*, and re-birth are misrepresented and caricatured, by the non-Indian members of their fold, who have no idea of the evil effects of the relaxing of traditional restrains. Christianity in India to-day hears the call of Hinduism. She may pay heed to it and follow or she may be deaf to it and refrain. But all signs indicate that she is choosing wisely. She is attempting to combine the best elements of Hinduism with the good points of Christianity, and if she succeeds, it is not India alone that will be the gainer by this Hindu Christianity. The spiritual life of the world will increase.

1. Modern Churchman October, 1922
2. IX. 30-31.
3. Luke xiii. 1-5.
4. Matthew xxv. 31-46.
5. Matthew xiii. 24-30; xxiv. 43; xii. 44; xiii. 45-46; xviii. 12 14-30; xxv. 1-13; xxii. 1-14.
6. See the Bhagavadagita, iv. 7-8; see also Professor Hogg's redemption from the World.
7. Romans viii. 92.
8. Browne : Litrary History of Persia, I. p. 439.
9. Luke xvi. 24.
10. John xvi. 12.
11. Mark. x. 18; John xiv. 28.
12. Luke xi. 19.
13. Revelation iii, 12.
14. Peter ii 23.
15. Justification and reconciliation, p. 387.
16. Luke xvi. 19-31.
17. Psalms ciii. 8.
18. Matthew vii. II.
19. Luke xxiii 1.43.

BUDDHISM

Buddha, the founder of the religion, is one of the noblest figures in the history of the world. A mass of legends has naturally grown round his person and there are some who even maintain that his whole life from birth to death was a legend. But it may be accepted that Buddha was a prince born to luxury who in the prime of life withdrew into solitude and sought truth through meditation.

It was an age of intellectual ferment. A congeries of conflicting theories and guesses accepted by some and denied by others, changing with men, reflecting the individual whims and wishes filled the air (see *Brahmajala sutta*). Struck by the clashing enthusiasms and the discordant systems, Buddha inferred the futility of metaphysical speculation. In the world of morals, ceremonial observances displaced moral obligations. In the sphere of religion, primitive superstitions lifted up their heads and were being exploited by the interested. Buddha declared that each man could gain salvation for himself without the mediation of priests or reference to Gods. Salvation did not depend on the acceptance of doubtful dogmas or doing deeds of darkness to appease angry deities, but on the perfection of character and devotion to the good. An aversion to metaphysical speculation, an absence of theological tendency and an ethical earnestness mark Buddha's teaching.

METAPHYSICS

The four truths which Buddha announced are that there is suffering, that it has a cause, that it can be suppressed and that there is a way to accomplish it. There is suffering because all things are transient. All being is in a state of perpetual becoming. Life is a series of becomings and extinctions. Whatever be the duration of any state of being, as brief as a flash of lightning or as long as a millennium, yet all is becoming. While Buddha distinguishes the momentary (ksanika) character of mental process from the impermanent (anitya) character of non-mental reality, later Buddhists regard all existence as momentary. Each single phenomenon is but a link in the chain, a transitory phase of evolution and the several chains constitute the one whole (dharmadhatu). Substances and souls are reduced to sequences and processes.

If we think of things rather than processes, we are dealing with unrealities. We build a seemingly stable universe through logical relations of substance and attribute, whole and part, cause and effect. These relations are true of our logical world and not of the real. We are naturally led to imagine a permanent core for things though it is an abstraction of thinking. We say it rains while there is no 'it' at all. There is nothing but movement, no doer but deed. We mistake continuity of becoming for identity of things. A child, a boy, a youth, a man and an old man are one. The seed and the tree are one. Continuous succession gives the appearance of an unbroken identity, even as a glowing stick whirled round gives the appearance of a complete circle. A useful convention makes us give names to the individual series. The identity of name persuades us to the thought of the identity of the inner reality.

The continuity of the world in the absence of a permanent substratum is explained by means of the principle of universal causation. A thing is only a dharma, a cause or a condition. "That being present this becomes; from the arising of that this arises; that being absent this does not become; from the cessation of that this ceases (Majjhima N. II 32). It is the doctrine of pratiyasamutpada or dependent origination. There is no being which changes; there is only a self-changing. The world series is not a series of extinctions and fresh creations. One state transmits its paccayasatti (causal energy) to the next. There is a cohesion of the past with the present which is broken up into a succession of before and after in an external treatment of nature.

The world of life and mōtion obeys a certain order (niyama). It is the presence of law in the world process which offers hope to man in distress. Regarding the nature of the world process, different views prevail. The chief tendency, however, is to look upon it as impermanent though not non-existent. There are suggestions of a purely subjectivist nature. "By the undoing of consciousness wholly remainderless all is melted away." The world is a product of ignorance and does not exist for the enlightened soul. Individual forms of the world are sometimes aid to be the manifestations of certain unconditioned reals. Composite substances disappear when true knowledge arises leaving behind the primary elements. Buddha was not interested so much in analysing the nature of the world of becoming as in helping us to get out of it. "It is not the time to discuss about fire for those who are actually in burning fire, but it is the time to escape from it."

The individual self is a compound where the component parts, mental (name) and material (rupa), are ever changing. Feeling (vedana), perception (samjna), disposition (samskara) and intelligence (vijnana) are the mental factors. Feeling refers to the affectional side, perception and intelligence to the cognitive and disposition to the volitional aspects of mental life. Intelligence sometimes functions as the self. We have no evidence of a permanent self. "When one says 'I' what he does is that he refers either to all the factors combined or any one of them and deludes himself that that was 'I'" (Samyutta N. III 130). While Buddha contents himself with a statement about the constituents of the empirical self without explicitly rejecting the existence of a permanent self, Nagasena dismisses the permanent self as an illegitimate abstraction and reduces the self of man to a unified complex exhibiting an unbroken historical continuity. As body is a name for a system of qualities, so soul is a name for the sum total of our mental states.

The conception of the soul retains enough meanig to make rebirth significant. The individual is not a haphazard succession of unconnected phenomena but is a living continuity. The reborn man is not the dead man; but he is not different from him. There is neither absolute identity nor absolute difference. There is persistent continuity as well as unceasing change. Each experience as it rises and passes leads up to, becomes or ends in another experience, moment or phase of life which sums up the whole past.

ETHICS AND RELIGION

Salvation which consists in the unmaking of ourselves is the goal of life. All forms of conduct which lead to it are regarded as good. The eightfold path - right belief, right aspirations, right speech, right conduct, right mode of livelihood, right effort, right-mindedness and right rapture - represents the morality of Buddhism. It is the middle way between the extremes of self-indulgence and self-mortification. It is intended to transform the whole life of man - intellectual, emotional and volitional.

The Institution of caste was in a confused state in the time of Buddha. He undermined the caste spirit by basing Brahminhood on conduct rather than on birth. He was not however a social reformer. His main interest was religion. Though professedly open to all, his religion was practically limited to the higher castes. He did not interfere with the domestic ritual which continued to be performed according to the Vedic rites. Buddha's mission was not so much to unveil the secrets of blessedness as to win men to its realisation. Nirvana literally means 'blowing out' or 'cooling'. It is the dying out of hot passion, the destruction of the fires of lust, hatred and ignorance. It is not to be confused with the night of nothingness. It is timeless existence full of "confidence, peace, calm, bliss, happiness, delicacy, purity, freshness" (Milinda, 11.2.9). Yamaka's view of nirvana as annihilation is repudiated as heresy (Samyutta N. III 103 ff). Since its nature is beyond the horizon of human thought, negative terms are used to describe Nirvana.

We need not regard Buddhism as an entirely fresh start with no roots in the past. It is a later phase of the general movement of thought of which the Upanishads are the earlier. The questions about ultimate reality, the nature of freedom and the permanent character of the self are not answered by Buddha. They are reserved issues on which he does not allow any speculation. he declines to answer Malunkya's questions on the ground that they do not help us in practical life (See also Dialogue of Vaccha). His silence on metaphysical issues is variously interpreted. Some of his early followers and modern interpreters take it negatively. They argue that Buddha did not believe in any permanent reality either cosmic or physical. Nirvana on this view is nothingness. Buddha, it is sometime urged, did not expound the negative view for fear that he might startle his followers. This view makes Buddha's philosophy incoherent and his character suspicious. There are positive statements made by Buddha which are inconsistent with this negative rationalism. Such a barren creed could not have appealed to theistically minded people of Buddha's time. Others hold that his silence was a cloak for his ignorance. He did not know the truth of things. This theory is implausible in view of Buddha's feeling that he was in possession of the truth and could lead men on to it. It is difficult to believe that Buddha himself was ignorant and wished his disciples to remain in ignorance. No thinking man could live without some sort of belief about ultimate values. It seems to be more reasonable to hold that Buddha accepted a positive idealism akin to the thought of the Upanishads, though he did not declare it as his opinion since he insisted on each one's realisation of the truth for oneself. He ignored metaphysical questions, as metaphysical wrangling distracts men from the main business of moral life. It has little to do with the attainment of sanctity which is more spiritual and inward than logical and theoretical. If we do not admit this view it will be difficult to account for the positive descriptions of the state of nirvana and Buddha's consistent refusal to deny the reality of an absolute beyond phenomena. The Benares sermon suggests strongly the reality of an absolute. In view of the obvious limits of the human understanding accepted by the Upanishads and Buddha, the latter refused to give positive accounts of it. But within the limits allowed by logic he describes the ultimate principle as dharma or righteousness. In the Upanishads, dharma (righteousness) and satya(truth) are identified. Since Buddha's main interest was ethical he emphasised the ethical nature of the absolute. Dharma takes the place of Brahman (D. N. III 232. On this question See Mind, 1926, pp. 158-174).

INDIAN PHILOSOPHY

I

PHILOSOPHICAL DEVELOPMENT

Throughout the history of Indian thought, the ideal of a world behind the ordinary world of human strivings, more real and more intangible, which is the true home of the spirit, has been haunting the Indian race. Man's never ceasing effort to read the riddle of the sphinx and raise himself above the level of the beast to a moral and spiritual height finds a striking illustration in India. We can watch the struggle for four millenniums (or longer, if the recent archaeological finds in Sind and the Punjab, which are withdrawing the shroud that hid the remote past, are to be taken into account). The naive belief that the world is ruled by the Gods of Sun and Sky, who watch from on high the conduct of men, whether it is straight or crooked; the faith that the Gods who can be persuaded by prayer or compelled by rites to grant our requests, are only the forms of the one Supreme; the firm conviction that the pure stainless spirit, to know whom is life eternal, is one with the innermost soul of man; the rise of materialism, scepticism and fatalism, and their supersession by the ethical systems of Buddhism and Jainism with their central doctrine that one can free one-self from all ill only by refraining from all evil, in thought, word and deed - God or no God; the liberal theism of the Bhagavadgita, which endows the all-soul with ethical in addition to metaphysical perfections; the logical scheme of the Nyaya, which furnishes the principal categories of the world of knowledge which are in use even to-day; the Vaiseshika interpretation of nature; the Samkhya speculations in science and psychology; the Yoga scheme of the pathway of perfection; the ethical and social regulations of the Mimamsa and the religious interpretations of the Supreme reality, as put forward by Sankara, Ramanuja, Madhva and Nimbarka, Vallabha and Jiva Gosvami - form a remarkable record of philosophical development in the history of the human race. Type succeeds type, school follows on school, in logical sequence. The life of the Indian was ever on the move, shaping itself as it grew, and changing from time to time in relation to its physical, social and cultural contexts. In the early stages the ancient Indians were doing everyting for the first time. They had practically no wisdom of the past to fall back upon. They had, moreover, enormous difficulties to contend with, which are now almost things of the past Inspite of these, their achievement in the realm of thougt and practice is a considerable one. But thc cycle is not complete, and the range of possible form is not exhausted; for the sphinx still smiles. Philosophy is yet in its infancy.

The survey of Indian thought, as of all thought, impresses one with the mystery and the immensity of existence as well as the beauty and the persistence of the human effort to understand it. The long procession of thinkers struggled hard to add some small piece to the temple of human wisdom, some fresh fragment to the ever incomplete sum of human knowledge. But human speculation falls short of the ideal, which it can neither abandon nor attain. We are far more conscious of the depth of the surrounding darkness than of the power to dispel it possessed by the flickering torches that we have the privilege to carry as the inheritors of a great past. After all the attempts of philosophers, we stand to-day in relation to the ultimate problems very near where we stood far away in the ages - where perhaps we shall ever stand as long as we are human, bound Prometheus-like to the rock of mystery by the chains of our finite mind.(1) The pursuit of philosophy is not, however, a vain endeavour. It helps us to feel the grip and the clanging of the chains. It sharpens the consciousness of human imperfection, and thus deepens the sense of perfection in us, which reveals the imperfection of our passing lives. That the world is not so transparent to our intellects as we could wish is not to be wondered at for the philosopher is only the lover of wisdom and not its possessor. It is not the end of the voyage that matters, but the voyage itself. To travel is a better thing than to arrive.

At the end of our course, we may ask whether the known facts of history support a belief in progress. Is the march of human thought a forward movement, or is it one of retrogression ? The sequence is not capricious and unmeaning. India believes in progress, for, as we have already said, the cycles are bound together by an organic tie. The inner thread of continuity is never cut. Even the revolutions that threaten to engulf the past help to restore it. Backward eddies serve rather to strengthen than retard the current. Epochs of decadence, like the recent past of this country, are in truth periods of transition from an old life to a new. The two currents of progress and decline are intermingled. At one stage the forces of progress press forward with a persistent sweep, at another the line sways to and fro, and sometimes the forces of retrogression seem to overwhelm those of progress, but on the whole the record is one of advance. It would be idle to deny that much has perished in the process. But few things are more futile than to rail against the course which the historical past has taken or weep over it. In any case, some other kind of development would have been worse. The more important thing is the future. We are able to see further than our predecessors, since we can climb on their shoulders. Instead of resting content with the foundations nobly laid in past, we must build a greater edifice in harmony with ancient endeavour as well as the modern outlook.

II

THE UNITY OF ALL SYSTEMS

The twin strands which in one shape or another run through all the efforts of the Indian thinkers are loyalty to tradition and devotion to truth. Every thinker recognises that the principles of his predecessors are stones built into the spiritual fabric, and, if they are traduced, one's own culture is defamed. A progressive people with a rich tradition cannot afford to neglect it, though it may contain elements which are not edifying. The thinkers try hard to explain, allegorise, alter and expurgate the traditional lore, since men's emotions are centred round it. The later Indian thinkers justify the different philosophical interpretations of the universe advanced by the earlier ones, and regard them as varying approximations to the truth as a whole. The different views are not looked upon as unrelated adventures of the human mind into the realm of the unknown or a collection of philosophical curiosities. They are regarded as the expression of a single mind, which has built up the great temple, though it is divided into numerous walls and vestibules, passages and pillars.

Logic and science, philosophy and religion are related organically. Every fresh epoch in the progress of thought has been inaugurated by a reform in logic. The problem of method, involving as it does an insight into the nature of human thought, is of great value. The Nyaya points out that no stable philosophy can be built except on the foundations of logic. The Vaiseshika warns us that all fruitful philosophy must take into account the constitution of physical nature. We cannot build in the clouds. Though physics and metaphysics are clearly distinct and cannot be blended, still a philosophic scheme must be in harmony with the results of natural science. But to extend to the universe at large what is true of the physical world would be to commit the fallacy of scientific metaphysics, and the Samkhya asks us to beware of that danger. The resources of nature cannot generate consciousness. We cannot reduce nature and psychological metaphysics attempt to do. Reality appears not only in science and in human life, but in religious experience, which is the subject matter of the Yoga system. The Purva Mimamsa and the Vedanta lay stress on ethics and religion. The relation between nature and mind is the supreme problem of philosophy which the Vedanta takes up. The saying, that the saints do not contradict one another, is true of philosophies also. The Nyaya-Vaiseshika realism, the Samkhya-Yoga dualism and the Vedanta monism do not differ as true and false but as more or less true.(2) They are adapted to the needs of the slow-witted (mandadhikari), the average intellect (madhyamadhikari), and the strong-minded (uttamadhikari) respectively. The different views are hewn out of one stone and belong to one whole, integral, entire and self-contaimed. No scheme of the universe can be regarded as complete, if it has not the different sides of logic and physics, psychology and ethics, metaphysics and religion. Every system of thought developed in India offered its own theory of knowledge, interpretation of nature and mind, ethics and religion. Our knowledge of the universe has grown enormously under the guidance of the natural sciences, and we cannot afford to be satisfied with any restricted outlook on life. The future attempts at philosophic construction will have to relate themselves to the recent advances of natural science and psychology.

III

PHILOSOPHY AND LIFE

Philosophy has for its function the ordering of life and the guidance of action. It sits at the helm and directs our course through the changes and chances of the world. When philosophy is alive, it cannot be remote from the life of the people. The ideas of thinkers are evolved in the process of their life history. We must learn not only to reverence them, but to acquire their spirit. The names of Vasishta and Visvamitra, Yajnavalkya and Gargi, Buddha and Mahavira, Gautama and Kanada, Kapila and Patanjali, Badarayana and Jaimini, Sankara and Ramanuja, are not merely themes for the historian but types of personality. With them philosophy is a world-view based on reflection and experience. Thought, when it thinks itself out to the end, becomes religion by being lived and tested by the supreme test of life. The discipline of philosophy is at the same time the fulfilment of a religious vocation.

IV

THE DECLINE OF PHILOSOPHY IN THE RECENT PAST

The evidence brought together in this work does not support the general criticism that the Indian mind has a fear of thinking. We cannot dismiss the whole progress of Indian thought with a sapient reference to the oriental mind, which is not sufficiently dry and virile to rise above grotesque imagination and puerile mythology. Yet there is much in the thought-history of the last three or four centuries to lend countenance to this charge. India is no longer playing her historic role as the vanguard of higher knowledge in Asia.(3) It seems to some that the river that has flowed down the centuries so strong and full is likely to end in a stagnant waste of waters. The philosophers, or rather the writers on philosophy of this period of decadence, profess to be votaries of truth, though they understand by it merely the pious sophistries or the sacrosanct hair-splittings of this or that school of dogmatics. These professional dialecticians imagine that the samll brook by their side, trickling away in the sand or evaporating in the fog, is the broad river of Indian philosophy.

A variety of causes have contributed to this result. The political changes brought about by the establishment of the Mohammadan supremacy turned men's minds into conservative moulds. In an age when individual self-assertion and private judgement threatened at every point to dissolve into anarchy the old social order and all stable conviction, the need for authoritative control was urgently felt. The Mohammadan conquest, with its propagandist work, and later the Christian missionary movement, attempted to shake the stability of Hindu society, and in an age deeply conscious of instability, authority naturally became the rock on which alone it seemed that social safety and ethical order could be reared. The Hindu, in the face of the clash of cultures, fortified himself with conventions and barred all entry to invading ideas. His society, mistrusting reason and weary of argument, flung itself passionately into the arms of an authority which stamped all free questioning as sin. Since then it has failed in loyalty to its mission. There were no longer any thinkers, but only scholars who refused to strike new notes, and were content to raise echoes of the old call. For some centuries they succeeded in deceiving themselves with a supposedly final theory. Philosophy became confused with the history of philosophy when the creative spirit had left her. It abdicated its function and remained wrapped up in its illusions. When it ceased to be the guide and the guardian of the general reason, it did a great wrong to itself. Many believed that their race had travelled long and far towards a goal at which it had at length arivred. They felt rather tired and inclined to rest. Even those who knew that they had not arrived, and saw the large tract of the country stretching into the future, were afraid of the unknown and its ordeals. The silences and the eternities cannot be questioned without peril by the weak of heart. The dizziness of the inquiry into the infinite is a vertigo which even mighty minds try to avoid, if they can. The strongest of human forces are subject to intervals of lethargy, and the philosophic impulse has had in these three or four centuries an attack of lethargy.

V

THE PRESENT SITUATION

To-day the great religions of the world and the different currents of thought have met on Indian soil. The contact with the spirit of the West has disturbed the placid contentment of recent times. The assimilation of a different culture has led to the impression that there are no official answers to ultimate problems It has shaken the faith in the traditional solutions, and has, in some degree, helped to a larger freedom and flexibility of thought. Tradition has become fluid again, and while some thinkers are busy rebuilding the house on ancient foundations, others want to remove the foundations altogether. The present age of transition is as full of interest as of anxiety.

During the recent past, India was comfortably moored in a backwater outside the full current of contemporary thought, but she is no longer isolated from the rest of the world. The historian of three or four centuries hence may have much to say on the issues of the intercourse between India and Europe, but as yet they lie hidden from our view. So far as India is concerned, we notice the broadening of men's range of experience, the growth of the critical temper and a sort of distate for mere speculation.

But there is another side to the picture. In the field of thought, as well as in that of action, the spirit of man is doomed to decay as much in anarchy as in bondage. There is not much to choose between the two, so far as culture and civilisation are concerned. Anarchy may mean material discomfort, economic ruin and social danger and bondage material comfort, economic stability and social peace. But it would be incorrect to confuse the standards of civilisation with economic welfare and maintenance of social order. It is easy to understand the feeling of the Indians of the beginning of the nineteenth centurey, who after generations of public strike and private suffering welcomed the British rule as the dawn of a golden age; but it should be equally easy to sympathise with the Indian feeling of the present day that the spirit of man craves, not comfort, but happiness, not peace and order, but life and liberty, not economic stability or equitable administration, but the right to work out one's own salvation even at the cost of infinite toil and tribulation. Even non-political virtues do not thrive in the absence of political autonomy. British rule has given India peace and security, but they are not ends in themselves. If we are to put first things first, then we must admit that economic stability and political security are only means, however valuable and necessary, to spiritual freedom. A bureaucratic despotism which forgets the spiritual ends, for all its integrity and enlightenment, cannot invigorate the peoples beneath her sway, and cannot therefore evoke any living response in them. When the founts of life are drying up, when the ideals for which the race stood for millenniums, the glow of consciousness, the free exercise of faculty, the play of life, the pleasure of mind and the fulness of peace, *pranaramam, mana-anandam, santi-samrddham,* are decaying, it is no wonder that the Indian is conscious only of the crushing burden and not of the lifted weight. It is no use speaking to him of the magnitude of Britain's work, for the verdict of history is passed on the spiritual quality of the achievement. If the leaders of recent generations have been content to be mere echoes of the past and not independent voices, if they have been intellectual middlemen and not original thinkers, this sterility is to no small extent due to the shock of the Western spirit and the shame of subjection. The British are aware of the deep-rooted causes of the present attitude of India, whatever it may be called, unrest, revolt or challenge. They tried to bring their civilisation, which they naturally regard as higher, to touch the Indians, and they felt that they should press on in the task of enlightenment and education, good in themselves, without any hesitation or cessation, of effort. But India has no sympathy with this policy of cultural imperialism. She tenaciously clings to her ancient customs which helped her to check the swell of passion, the blindness of temper and the thrust of desire. One who is acquainted with the history of her past can sympathise with her anxiety to dwell in her own spiritual house, for "each man is the master of his own house."(4) Political subjection which interferes with this inner freedom is felt as a gross humiliation. The cry for Swaraj is the outer expression of the anxiety to preserve the provinces of the soul.

Yet the future is full of promise. If India gains freedom within, then the Western spirit will be a great help to the Indian mind. Hindu thought never developed a Monroe doctrine in matters of culture. Even in the ancient times when India grew enough spiritual food to satisfy her own people, there is no recorded age when she was not ready and eager to appreciate the products of other people's imagination. In her great days India conformed to the wisdom of the Athenians, of whom Pericles said : "We listen gladly to the opinions of others and do not turn our faces on those who disagree with us." Our fear of outside influence is proportioned to our own weakness and want of faith in ourselves. To-day, it is true, we bear lines of sorrow in our face and our hair is grey with age. The thoughtful among us have a brooding uneasiness of soul, some are even steeped in pessimism, and so have become intellectual hermits. The non co-operation with Western culture is a passing episode due to unnatural circumstances. In spite of it, there are attempts to understand and appreciate the spirit of Western culture. If India assimilates the valuable elements in the Western civilisation, it will be only a repetition of parallel processes which happened a number of times in the history of Indian thought.

Those who are untouched by the Western influence are for a large part intellectual and moral aristocrats, who are indifferent to political issues, and adopt a gospel not of confident hope but of resignation and detachment. They think that they have little to learn or to unlearn and that they do their duty with their gaze fixed on the eternal Dharma of the past. They realise that other forces are at work, which they cannot check or control, and ask us to face the storms and disillusionment of life with the unruffled calm of self-respect. This was the class which in better times was more elastic and was ever renewing the attempts to reconcile rational philosophy with revealed religion. It had always explained and defended the faith in the face of heretics and unbelievers, and had recourse to the allegorical method as the instrument of theological intepretation.

The thinkers of India are the inheritors of the great tradition of faith in reason. The ancient seers desired not to copy but to create. They were ever anxious to win fresh fields for truth and answer the riddles of experience, which is ever changing and therefore new. The richness of the inheritance never served to enslave their minds. We cannot simply copy the solutions of the past, for history never repeats itself. What they did in their generation need not be done over again. We have to keep our eyes open, find out our problems and seek the inspiration of the past in solving them. The spirit of truth never clings to its forms but ever renews them. Even the old phrases are used in a new way. The philosophy of the present will be relevant to the present and not to the past. It will be as original in its form and its content as the life which it interprets. As the present is continuous with the past, so there will be no breach of continuity with the past.

One of the arguments of the conservatives is that truth is not affected by time. It cannot be superseded, any more than the beauty of the sunset or a mother's love for a child. Truth may be immutable, but the form in which it is embodied consists of elements which admit of change. We may take our spirit from the past, for the germinal ideas are yet vital, but the body and the pulse must be from the present. It is forgotten that religion, as it is to-day, is itself the product of ages of change; and there is no reason why its forms should not undergo fresh changes so long as the spirit demands it. It is possible to remain faithful to the letter and yet pervert the whole spirit. If the Hindu leaders of two thousand years ago, who had less learning and more light, could come on earth again after all these centuries, they would seldom find their true followers among those who have never deviated from the most literal interpretations of their views.(5) To-day a great mass of accretions have accumulated, which are choking up the stream and the free life of spirit. To say that the dead forms, which have no vital truth to support them, are too ancient and venerable to be tampered with, only prolongs the suffering of the patient who is ailing from the poison generated by the putrid waste of the past. The conservative mind must open itself to the necessity of change. Since it is not sufficiently alive to this need, we find in the realm of philosophy a strange mixture of penetrating sagacity and unphilosophical confusion. The chief energies of the thinking Indians should be thrown into the problems of how to disentangle the old faith from its temporary accretions, how to bring religion into line with the spirit of science, how to meet and interpret the claims of temperament and individuality, how to organise the divergent influences on the basis of the ancient faith.

But, unfortunately, some of the parisads are engaged not with these problems but those suited for the society of Antiquarians. It has become the tilting-ground of the specialists. The religious education of the nation. is not undertaken on broad lines. It is not seen that spiritual inheritance cannot be any longer the monopoly of a favoured few. Ideas are forces, and they must be broadcasted, if the present ageing to death is to be averted. It would be indeed strange if the spirit of the Upanishads, the Gita and the Dialogues of Buddha, that could touch the mind to such fine issues, should have lost its power over man. If, before it is too late, there is a reorganisation of national life there is a turure for Indian thought; and one cannot tell what flowers may yet bloom, what fruits may yet ripen on the hardy old trees.

While those who have not yet been subjected to the influence of Western culture are conservatives in all matters of thought and practice, there are some among those educated in Western ways of thinking who adopt a despairing philosophy of naturalistic rationalism and ask us to get rid of the weight of the past. These are intolerant of tradition and suspicious of the alleged wisdom of age. This attitude of the "progressives" is easily understood. The spiritual heritage of the race has not protected India from the invader and the spoiler. It seems to have played her false and betrayed her into the present state of subjection. These patriots are eager to imitate the material achievements of Western states, and tear up the roots of the ancient civilisation, so as to make room for the novelties imported from the West. Till the other day Indian thought was not a subject of study in the Indian Universities, and even now its place in the philosophical curricula of the Universities is insignificant. Suggestions of the inferiority of Indian culture permeate the whole educational atmosphere. The policy inaugurated by Macaulay, with all its cultural value, is loaded on one side. While it is so careful as not to make us forget the force and vitality of Western culture, it has not helped us to love our own culture and refine it where necessary. In some cases, Macaulay's wish is fulfilled, and we have educated Indians who are 'more English than the English themselves,' to quote his well-known words. Naturally some of these are not behind the hostile foreign critic in their estimate of the history of Indian culture. They look upon India's cultural evolution as one dreary scene of discord, folly and superstition. One of their number recently declared that, if India is to thrive and flourish, England must be her "spiritual mother" and Greece her "spiritual grandmother." Albeit, since he has no faith in religion, he does not propose the displacement of Hinduism by Christianity. These victims of the present age of disillusion and defeat tell us that the love of Indian thought is a nationalist foible, if not a pore of the highbrows.

It is a bewildering phenomenon that, just when India is ceasing to appear grotesque to Western eyes, she is beginning to appear so to the eyes of some of her own sons. The West tried its best to persuade India that its philosophy is absurd, its art puerile, its poetry uninspired, its religion grotesque and its ethics barbarous. Now that the West is feeling that its judgement is not quite correct, some of us are insisting that it was wholly right. While it is true that it is difficult in an age of reflection to push men back into an earlier stage of culture and save them from the dangers of doubt and the disturbing power of dialectic, we should not forget that we can build better on foundations already laid than by attempting to substitute a completely new structure of morality, of life and of ethics. We cannot cut ourselves off from the springs of our life. Philosophical schemes, unlike geometrical constructions, are the products of life. The heritage of our history is the food that we have to absorb on pain of inanition.

The conservatives are convinced of the glory of the ancient heritage and the godlessness of modern culture; the radicals are equally certain of the futility of the ancient heritage and the value of naturalistic rationalism. There is much to be said for these views; but the history of Indian thought, when rightly studied, will lead us to regard the two as equally defective. Those who condemn Indian culture as useless are ignorant of it, we those who commend it as perfect are ignorant of any other. The radicals and the conservatives, who stand for the new hope and the old learning, must come closer and understand each other. We cannot live by ourselves in a world where aircraft and steamships, railways and telegraphs are linking all men together into a living whole. Our system of thought must act and react on the world progress. Stagnant systems like pools, breed obnoxious growths while flowing rivers constantly renew their waters from fresh springs of inspiration. There is nothing wrong in absorbing the culture of other peoples; only we must enhance, raise and purify the elements we take over, fuse them with the best in our own. The right procedure regarding the fusing together of the different elements tossed from outside into the natioal crucible, is indicated roughtly in the writings of Gandhi and Tagore, Aurobindo Ghosh and Bhagavan Das. In them we see that faint promise of a great future, some signs of a triumph over scholasticism, as well as response to the discovery of a great culture. While drawing upon the fountains of humanist idealism in India's past, they show a keen appreciation of Western thought. They are anxious to reseek the ancient fountain-head and direct its waters to irrigate, through pure and uncontaminated conduits, lands which hunger and thirst. But the future which we wish to see is practically non-existent. With the slackening of the political excitement, which is absorbing the energies of some of the best minds of India, with the increasing insistence on the study of Indian thought in the new Universities, which the old ones are following most reluctantly, the dawn may break. The forces of the conservatism, which prefers the life that was to the life that will be, are not likely to gain any strength in the days to come.

The problem facing Indian Philosophy to-day is whether it is to be reduced to a cult, restricted in scope and with no application to the present facts or whether it is to be made alive and real, so as to become what it should be, one of the great formative elements in human progress, by relating the immensely increased knowledge of modern science to the ancient ideals of India's philosophers. All signs indicate that the future is bound up with the latter alternative. Loyalty to the spirit of the previous systems of thought, as well as the mission of philosophy, requires us to possess an outlook that always broadens. Indian philosophy acquires a meaning and a justification for the present only if it advances and ennobles life. The past course of Indian philosophic development encourages us in our hope. The great thinkers, Yajnavalkya and Gargi, Buddha and Mahavira, Gautama and Kapila, Sankara and Ramanuja, Madhva and Vallabha, and scores of others are India's grandest title to existence, a clear testimony of her dignity as a nation with a soul, the proof that she may yet rise above herself and the pledge of this supreme possibility.

1. "No one," exclaims Xenophanes, 'has attained complete certainty in respect to the gods and to that which I call universal nature, nor will anyone ever attain it. Nay, even if a man happened to light on the truth, he would not know that he did so, for appearance is spread over all things" (Gomperz : Greek Thinkers, vol. i. p. 164).
2. Madhava S.D.S.; Madhusudana Sarasvati's prasthanabheda; Vijnanabhiksu's Introduction to S.P.B. Cp. Kant : "We are in a way maintaining the honour of human reason when we reconcile it with itself in the different persons of acute thinkers and discover the truth, which is never entirely missed by men of such thoroughness, even if they directly contradict each other" (quoted in J. Ward : A Study of Kant, p. 11. n. 1).
3. Regarding China's debt to India, professor Liang Chi Che says : "India taught us to embrace the idea of absolute freedom, that fundamental freedom of mind, which enables it to shake off all the fetters of past tradition an habit as well as the present customs of a particular age - that spiritual freedom which casts off the enslaving forces of material exixtence . . . India also taught us the idea of absolute love, that pure love towards all living beings which eliminates all obsessions of jealousy, anger, impatience, disgust and emulation, which expresses itself in deep pity and sympathy for the foolish, the wicked and the sinful -- that absolute love which recognises the inseparability between all beings." He goes on to explain the contributions of India to Chinese literature and art, music and architecture, painting and sculpture, drama, poetry and fiction, astronomy and medicine, educanal method and social organisations. *See Visvabharati Quarterly*, October 1924. The influence of India on Burma and Ceylon, Japan and Corea, is well known.
4. Sarvas sve grhe raja. Every mam is the lord in his own house.
5. Cp. Aurbindo Ghosh : "If an ancient Indian of the time of the Upanishad, of the Buddha, or the later classical age were to be set down in modern India . . he would see his race clinging to forms and shells and rags of the past and missing nine-tenths of its nobler meaning . . . he would be amazed by the extent of the mental poverty, the immobility, the static repetition, the cessation of science, the long sterility of art, the comaprative feebleness of the creative intuition" (Arya, v. p. 424).